MW01235043

LESSWRONG

Refining the art of human rationality

Foreword

Each year, the LessWrong community votes on the best posts from the previous year, to see which posts have stood the tests of time.

In 2020, the highest ranked post was Catherine Olsson's announcement of microCOVID.org, a calculator for evaluating COVID risk. MicroCOVID is one of the clearest success stories of the 'rationalist mindset' that I know of. Creating it involved research during the early pandemic, when information was scarce, and time was of the essence – a classic situation where the traditional scientific process is inadequate and LessWrong-style rationality tools are valuable. It also required a quantitative mindset, and willingness to assign numbers to risks and make tradeoffs.

But microCOVID.org is most interesting to me as a tool for coordination. It doesn't just let individuals make better life choices. Microcovid changed the entire covid coordination landscape by relaxing a constraint. Previously, if you lived with people with varying covid-caution preferences, and you wanted to hang out with someone from another house of people with varying covid-caution preferences... your only option was to have fairly involved negotiations on a case-by-case basis. Many people I know grew exhausted from negotiating, and gave up on trying to visit their friends. The microCOVID tool gave people a simplified "risk budget", letting them do whatever activities made sense to them as long as they didn't overspend.

"Negotiation energy" was a limiting resource, and microcovid.org made negotiation radically cheaper. It also opened up entirely new options, like "create a household microCOVID tax" (some houses decided that you could do whatever activities you wanted, you just had to pay other housemates $1 per microcovid).

The proximate inspiration for the theme of this book (and included herein) are John Wentworth's posts "Coordination as Scarce Resource", "Transportation as Constraint", and "Interfaces as Scarce Resource." Other posts explore the nature of particular constraints that society faces – Zvi's posts on "Simulacra Levels and their Interactions," "The Road to Mazedom," and "Motive Ambiguity" each spell out how and why some communication is systematically distorted. And while they don't give us a solution, they help ask a question – what would need to change, in order for society to coordinate at scale, without incentivizing distorted communication?

Many failures of our civilization are attributed to bad actors, selfishness, shortsightedness, or similar issues. How many coordination failures could actually be overcome if we simply had better tools to relax the constraints, and thereby enable coordination?

Illustrations in this book were created by AI, using Midjourney version 4.
Each image is based loosely on the title or concepts in each post.

Coordination & Constraint

Coordination as a scarce resource

Let's start with a few examples of very common real-world coordination problems.

- The marketing department at a car dealership posts ads for specific cars, but the salespeople don't know which cars were advertised, causing confusion when a customer calls in asking about a specific car. There's no intentional information-hoarding; it's just that the marketing and sales people don't sit next to each other or talk very often. Even if the info were shared, it would need to be translated to a format usable by the salespeople.

- Various hard problems in analysis of large-scale biological data likely have close analogues in econometrics. The econometricians have good methods to solve the problems and would probably be quite happy to apply those methods to biological data, and the bio experimentalists would love some analytic help. But these people hardly ever talk to each other and use different language for the same things anyway.

- When the US invaded Grenada in the '80s, the marines occupied one side of the island and the army occupied the other. Their radios were not compatible, so if an army officer needed to contact their counterpart in the marines, they had to walk to the nearest pay phone and get routed through Fort Bragg on commercial telephone lines.

- Various US intelligence agencies had all of the pieces necessary to stop the 9/11 attacks. There were agencies which knew something was planned for that day and knew who the actors were. There were agencies which knew the terrorists were getting on the planes. There were agencies which could have moved to stop them, but unfortunately, the fax(!) from the agencies which knew what was happening wasn't checked in time.

- There are about 300 million people in the US. If I have a small company producing doilies, chances are there are plenty of people in the US alone who'd love my doilies and be happy to pay for them. But it's hard to figure out exactly which people those are, and even once that's done it's hard to get them a message showing off my product. And even if all that works out, if the customers really want a slightly different pattern, it's hard for them to communicate back to me what they want - even if I'd be happy to make it.

So coordination problems are a constraint to production of all kinds of economic value. How taut are those constraints?

Well, let's look at the market price of relaxing coordination constraints. In other words: how much do people/companies get paid for solving coordination problems?

When I think of people whose *main* job is to solve coordination problems, here are some occupations which spring to mind:

- Entrepreneurs' main job is to coordinate salespeople, engineers, designers, marketers, investors, customers, regulators, suppliers, shippers, etc.

- Managers' main job is to coordinate between their bosses, underlings, and across departments

- Investment bankers coordinate between investors, companies, lawyers, and a huge number of people within each of those organizations

- Real estate developers coordinate between builders, landowners, regulators, renters, and investors

Note that all of these are occupations typically associated with very high pay. Even more to the point: within each of these occupations, people who solve more complicated coordination problems (e.g. between more people) tend to make more money. Even at the small end, the main difference between an employee and a freelancer is that the freelancer has to solve their own coordination problem (i.e. find people who want their services); freelancers make lots of money mainly when they are very good at solving this problem.

Similarly with companies. If we go down the list of tech unicorns, most (though not all) of them solve coordination problems as their primary business model:

- Google matches company websites to potentially interested users

- Facebook is a general-purpose coordination platform

- Amazon and Ebay are general-purpose marketplaces: they match buyers to sellers

- Uber/Lyft are more specialized marketplaces

Again: solving coordination problems at scale offers huge amounts of money.

This suggests that coordination problems are *very* taut constraints in today's economy.

It's not hard to imagine *why* coordination problems would be very taut today. Over the past ~50 years, global travel/transportation has gone from rare to ordinary, and global communication has become cheap and ubiquitous. Geographical constraints have largely been relaxed, and communication/information processing constraints have largely been relaxed. The number of people we *could* potentially coordinate with has expanded massively as a result - a small doily business can now sell to a national or even global customer base; a phone app can connect any willing driver in a city to any paying rider.

Yet human brains have not changed much, even as the number of people we interact with skyrockets past Dunbar's number. It's hard for humans to coordinate with thousands - let alone billions - of other humans. The coordination constraint remains, so as other constraints relax, it becomes more taut.

What Would This Model Predict?

One prediction: suppose I've decided to become a freelancer/consultant. I can invest effort in becoming better at my object-level craft, or I can invest effort in becoming better at solving my coordination problem - e.g. by exploring marketing channels or studying my target market. Which of these will make more money? Probably the latter - coordination constraints are *very* taut, so there's lots of money to be made by relaxing them.

More generally, when evaluating new business ideas, questions on my short list include:

• How will this business find people who would want to buy the product?

• How will this business make those people aware of the product?

To the extent that coordination is an unusually taut constraint, answers to these questions will be the main determinant of business profitability - even more so than product quality.

Coming from a different direction, when considering a business idea, we should ask how many different kinds of people this business needs to coordinate. At one point, I worked at a mortgage startup where the list of internal departments included marketing, sales, underwriting, legal, and capital markets on the mortgage side; plus design, engineering, and ops on the tech side; and on top of that we had to interface to at least a dozen external companies on a regular basis. Coordination is *the* primary constraint at a company like that.

Yet another direction: if coordination constraints are very taut, then we expect adoption of technology which makes coordination easier. One form of this is outlined in From Personal to Prison Gangs: people make *themselves* easier to coordinate with by following standardized patterns of behavior and fitting into standard molds. For instance, in large organizations (where more people need to coordinate) we tend to see group-based identity: rather than understanding what John or Allan does, people understand what lawyers or developers do. Interactions between people become more standardized and roles become more rigid - these are solutions to coordination problems. Such solutions entail large tradeoffs, but coordination constraints are very taut, so large tradeoffs are accepted.

Conversely, if we want a world with less pressure to standardize behavior, then we need some other way to relax coordination constraints - some technology which helps people coordinate at scale without needing to standardize behavior as much. Such technology would probably see wide adoption, and potentially make quite a lot of money as well.

Summary

I often hear people say they'd like object-level skill/effort to be rewarded more than marketing/sales, or they'd like to see less pressure to standardize behavior, or they'd like the world to be more individualized and identity to be less group-based. To the extent that we buy the picture here, all of these phenomena are solutions to coordination problems. Society rewards marketing over object-level skill and tries to standardize behavior, because coordination constraints are extremely taut.

If we want the world to look less like that, then we need alternative scalable technologies to solve coordination problems.

Endnotes

(1) John S Wentworth. From Personal to Prison Gangs: Enforcing Prosocial Behavior. 24th Jan 2019.

John S Wentworth

Transportation as a constraint

Imagine it's late autumn of 332 BC. You're Alexander the Great, and your armies are marching toward Egypt from Gaza. There's just one little problem: you need to cross the Sinai peninsula - 150 miles of hot, barren desert. How will you carry food and water for the troops?

Dark triangle on the left is the Nile river delta in Egypt; dark chunk in the upper right is Israel. The big desert peninsula between them is the Sinai.

Option 1: carry it

A physically-active human needs about 3 lbs of food per day. (Modern hikers can probably find lighter calorie-dense foodstuffs, but we're talking ancient history here.) Water requirements vary; 5 lbs is a minimum, but the US Army Quartermaster Corps recommends 20 lbs/day when marching through a hot desert. Alexander's army crossed the desert in 7 days. Food might be reasonable, but to carry the water would mean 7*20 = 140 lbs per person, plus 50+ lbs of armor, weapons, etc.

When I go hiking, I aim for a 20-30 lb pack. US marines are apparently expected to be able to carry 150 lbs for 9 miles[1]—quite a bit less than the 20+ miles/day Alexander's army managed, and with no comment on how long the marine in question might need to rest afterwards. (Also, I'm not sure I trust that source - 150 lbs for 9 miles sounds unrealistic to me, and if it's true then I'm *very* impressed by marines.)

Suffice to say that carrying that much water across that much desert is not a realistic option, even if we drink it along the way.

Option 2: horses

A horse consumes 20 lbs of food (half of which may be forage) and 80 lbs of water per day. In exchange, it can carry about 200 lbs (surprisingly, my source claims that horses can carry more than they can pull). Of course, that 200 lbs has to include the horse's own food and water, plus whatever useful load it's carrying. So, marching through a desert, a horse can only transport (200 lbs)/(80+20 lbs/day) = 2 days of supplies *for itself*, and that's before whatever useful things actually need to be transported.

In other words, there's a hard upper limit on how far goods can be transported by horse without refilling supplies along the way. That limit is around 2 days travel time without any refill, 10 days if there's plenty of fresh water along the route, or 20 days if there's both water and forage. At 20 miles/day, that's 40, 200, or 400 miles. Realistically, if we want the number of horses to be reasonable, the limit is more like half that much—20 miles, 100 miles, or 200 miles, respectively.

So horses also won't work.

Option 2.5: camels or other pack animals

Contrary to popular image, camels actually need more water than horses. They can go a couple days without, but then need to fill up all at once. They can also carry a bit more weight, but they eat more food. At the end of the day, the numbers end up quite similar.

Mules also end up with similar numbers, and cattle are generally worse.

Option 3: ships

Assuming the army marches along the coast, a supply fleet can sail alongside. At the time, a single large merchant ship could carry 400 tons - in other words, as much as about 4000 horses. Presumably the ship would cost a lot less than the horses, too.

Well then, there's our answer. Ships are clearly a vastly superior way to move goods. Range is a non-issue, capacity is far larger, and they're far cheaper. They're perfect for crossing the Sinai, which runs right along the coast anyway.

Fast forward a few years to 327 BC, and Alexander is marching his armies back from India. He plans to cross the Gedrosian desert, along the coast of modern-day Pakistan and Iran. The plan is much like the Sinai: a supply fleet will sail alongside the army. Unfortunately, neither Alexander nor his commanders knows about the monsoons: across most of south Asia, the wind blows consistently southwest for half the year, and consistently northeast for the other half. There is nothing like it in the Mediterranean. And so, Alexander marches out expecting the fleet to catch up as soon as the winds turn—not realizing that the winds will not turn for months. Three quarters of his soldiers die in the desert.

Thus end the campaigns of Alexander.

Generalization

The above numbers are drawn from Donald Engels' book Alexander the Great and the Logistics of Macedonian Army. But it tells us a lot more about the world than just the logistics of one particular ancient army.

First, this highlights the importance of naval dominance in premodern warfare. A fleet was a far superior supply train, capable of moving a high volume of food and water over long distance at relatively low cost. Without a fleet, transport of food became expensive at best, regular resupply became a strategic necessity, and long routes through arid terrain became altogether impassable. Destroying an enemy's fleet meant starving the army. Likewise, controlling ports wasn't just for show—without a port, feeding the army became a serious problem.

Another interesting insight into premodern warfare: away from friendly seas and rivers, the only way to keep an army fed was to either seize grain from enemies, or buy it from allies, either of whom needed to already be nearby. In Alexander's case, deals were often struck to establish supply caches along the army's intended route.

An interesting exercise: to what extent was transportation a binding constraint on the size of premodern towns/cities? (One number you may want: a book by Braudel$_2$ estimates that 5000 square meters of land growing wheat would provide one person-year of food, not accounting for crop rotation.)

Modern Day

Today we have trains and trucks and roads, so the transportation constraint has relaxed somewhat. But here's an interesting comparison: a modern 18-wheeler in the US is legally limited to haul 40 tons, while a panamax ship could carry about 50k tons through the canal (prior to the opening of the new locks in 2016). That's a ratio of a bit over 1000 - surprisingly similar to the ship/horse ratio of antiquity, especially considering the much larger new-panamax and super-panamax ships also in use today.

Can we get a quick-and-dirty feel for tautness of the transportation constraint today? Here are a few very different angles:

- The USDA study, How Transportation Costs Affect Fresh Fruit and Vegetable Prices shows rates on produce transport, typically about 7-20 cents per pound (see figure 6). The Smart & Final grocery store near me sells the cheaper produce items looked at in that study (bell peppers, cantaloupes, tomatoes, oranges) for 70-100 cents per pound, so transport alone is roughly 10-20% of the cost-to-consumer. [3]

- What about transporting humans? Average commute in the US is ~30 minutes each way; driving is usually in the 20-30 minute range, while public transit is usually 30-50. Assuming 8 hr workdays, that means commutes are typically ~10-20% of our work-hours. [4]

- The bureau of transportation estimates transport at 5.6% of the US economy for a very narrow measure, or 8.9% with a broader measure (though this still excludes non-market transport costs like e.g. commute time). [5]

My interpretation: the transportation constraint becomes taut when it accounts for 10-20% of cost. If it's less than that, it usually doesn't limit production - we see plenty of goods which aren't transportation-dependent or which are higher-value-per-weight, and the transportation constraint is generally slack for those. But once transportation hits about 10-20%, people start looking for alternatives, i.e. producing the goods somewhere else or using alternative goods. Obviously this is not based on very much data, but I find it intuitively plausible.

Compared to ancient times, transportation constraints have obviously relaxed quite a lot. Yet qualitatively, the world today still does not look like a world of fully slack transportation constraints. To wrap up, let's discuss what that would look like.

Extreme Slackness

In my previous essay Material Goods as an Abundant Resource[6], I discussed the world of the duplicator—a device capable of copying any item placed on it. In such a world, material scarcity is removed as an economic constraint—all material constraints are completely slack.

What would be a corresponding sci-fi device for transportation constraints, and what would that world look like?

I suggest portals: imagine we can create pairs of devices capable of transporting things from one device to the other, across any distance, at the speed of light. (We could instead imagine teleporters, removing the need for a pre-installed device at either end, but then the entire discussion would be about security.) What does the world of the portal look like?

First, there's complete geographical decoupling of production from consumption. People have no need to live near where they work: companies can put offices and factories wherever real estate is cheap. We can enjoy miles of wilderness on the back porch and a downtown district on the front porch; a swimming pool can open right into the ocean. Buying direct from the farm or factory is standard for most material goods.

What are now tourist destinations would become options for an evening activity. Disneyworld would sell a park-hopper ticket that includes Disneyland California, Paris, and Shanghai, but the price of that ticket would be high enough to prevent the parks from becoming unpleasantly crowded—probably quite a bit more expensive than today, though possibly cheaper than today's flights to Orlando.

Obviously roads would cease to exist. Huge amounts of land would revert from asphalt to wilderness, but buildings would also be much more spread out. Buildings would be built close together more for show than for function; e.g.: to provide the ambiance of a downtown or a community to those who want it. Physical life, in general, would look more like the structure of the internet rather than the structure of geography; "cities" would be clusters very spread out in space but very tightly connected via the portal network. Filter bubbles would be a much more physically tangible phenomenon.

Geographically-defined governments would likely be replaced by some other form of government - governments based around access to portal hubs/networks are one natural possibility. Security would be a priority, early on—carrying an unauthorized portal into an area would earn a faceful of high explosives. On the other hand, it would be hard to prevent a high degree of mobility between areas controlled by different governments; the implications for government behavior are conceptually similar to seasteading[7].

The structure of space near portal networks would be different in a big-O sense; the amount of space at a distance of about r would increase exponentially, rather than like $r2$. A nuclear warhead could go off five hundred feet away and you'd feel a breeze through a fast-branching portal network. On the other hand, viruses could spread much more rapidly.

Anyway, at this point we're getting into specifics of portals, so I'll cut off the speculation. The point is: if transportation continues to get cheaper and more efficient over time, then we will converge to the world of the portal, or at least something like it. The details do matter—portals are different from teleportation or whatever might actually happen—but any method of fully relaxing transportation constraints will have qualitatively similar results, to a large extent.

Endnotes

(1) David Hambling. The Overloaded Soldier: Why U.S. Infantry Now Carry More Weight Than Ever. Dec 2018.

(2) Fernand Braudel. Civilization and Capitalism, 15th–18th Century, Vol. I: The Structure of Everyday Life (Civilization & Capitalism, 15th–18th Century). 23rd Dec 1992. (Page 121).

(3) Richard Volpe, Edward Roeger, and Ephraim Leibtag. How Transportation Costs Affect Fresh Fruit and Vegetable Prices. Nov 2013.

(4) Jeff Desjardins. Visualizing the Average Commute Time in U.S. States and Cities. April 2018.

(5) Bureau of Transportation Statistics. 2018.

(6) John S. Wentworth. Material Goods as an Abundant Resource. 25th Jan 2020.

(7) Wayne Gramlich, Patri Friedman, and Andrew House. Getting Serious about SeaSteading. 2002.

John S Wentworth

Interfaces as a scarce resource

Outline

- The first three sections (Don Norman's Fridge, Interface Design, and When And Why Is It Hard?) cover what I mean by "interface," what it looks like for interfaces to be scarce, and the kinds of areas where they tend to be scarce.

- The next four sections apply these ideas to various topics:

  - Why AR is much more difficult than VR

  - AI-alignment from an interface-design perspective

  - Good interfaces as a key bottleneck to creation of markets

  - Cross-department interfaces in organizations

Don Norman's Fridge

Don Norman (known for popularizing the term "affordance" in The Design of Everyday Things[1]) offers a story about the temperature controls on his old fridge:

> I used to own an ordinary, two-compartment refrigerator—nothing very fancy about it. The problem was that I couldn't set the temperature properly. There were only two things to do: adjust the temperature of the freezer compartment and adjust the temperature of the fresh food compartment. And there were two controls, one labeled "freezer," the other "refrigerator." What's the problem?

> Oh, perhaps I'd better warn you. The two controls are not independent. The freezer control also affects the fresh food temperature, and the fresh food control also affects the freezer.

The natural human model of the refrigerator is: there's two compartments, and we want to control their temperatures independently. Yet the fridge, apparently, does not work like that. Why not? Norman:

> In fact, there is only one thermostat and only one cooling mechanism. One control adjusts the thermostat setting, the other the relative proportion of cold air sent to each of the two compartments of the refrigerator.

It's not hard to imagine why this would be a good design for a cheap fridge: it requires only one cooling mechanism and only one thermostat. Resources are saved by not duplicating components—at the cost of confused customers.

The root problem in this scenario is a mismatch between the structure of the machine (one thermostat, adjustable allocation of cooling power) and the structure of what-humans-want (independent temperature control of two compartments). In order to align the behavior of the fridge with the behavior humans want, somebody, at some point, needs to do the work of translating between the two structures. In Norman's fridge example, the translation is botched, and confusion results.

We'll call whatever method/tool is used for translating between structures an interface. Creating good methods/tools for translating between structures, then, is interface design.

Interface Design

In programming, the analogous problem is *API design*: taking whatever data structures are used by a software tool internally, and figuring out how to present them to external programmers in a useful, intelligible way. If there's a mismatch between the internal structure of the system and the structure of what-users-want, then it's the API designer's job to translate. A "good" API is one which handles the translation well.

User interface design is a more general version of the same problem: take whatever structures are used by a tool internally, and figure out how to present them to external users in a useful, intelligible way.

Conceptually, the only difference from API design is that we no longer assume our users are programmers interacting with the tool via code. We design the interface to fit however people use it—that could mean handles on doors$_2$, or buttons and icons in a mobile app, or the temperature knobs on a fridge.

Economically, interface design is a necessary input to make all sorts of things economically useful. How scarce is that input? How much are people willing to spend for good interface design?

My impression is: a lot. There's an entire category of tech companies whose business model is:

- Find a software tool or database which is very useful but has a bad interface

- Build a better interface to the same tool/database

- …

- Profit

This is an especially common pattern among small but profitable software companies; it's the sort of thing where a small team can build a tool and then lock in a small number of very loyal high-paying users. It's a good value prop—you go to people or businesses who need to use X, but find it a huge pain, and say "here, this will make it much easier to use X". Some examples:

- Companies which interface to government systems to provide tax services, travel visas, patenting, or business licensing

- Companies which set up websites, Salesforce, corporate structure, HR services, or shipping logistics for small business owners with little relevant expertise

- Companies which provide graphical interfaces for data, e.g. website traffic, sales funnels, government contracts, or market fundamentals

Even bigger examples can be found outside of tech, where humans themselves serve as an interface. Entire industries consist of people serving as interfaces.

What does this look like? It's the entire industry of tax accountants, or contract law, or lobbying. It's any industry where you could just do it yourself in principle, but the system is complicated and confusing, so it's useful to have an expert around to translate the things-you-want into the structure of the system.

In some sense, the entire field of software engineering is an example. A software engineer's primary job is to translate the things-humans-want into a language understandable by computers. People use software engineers because talking to the engineer (difficult though that may be) is an easier interface than an empty file in Jupyter.

These are not cheap industries. Lawyers, accountants, lobbyists, programmers—these are experts in complicated systems, and they get paid accordingly. The world spends large amounts of resources using people as interfaces—indicating that these kinds of interfaces are a very scarce resource.

When And Why Is It Hard?

Don Norman's work is full of interesting examples and general techniques for accurately communicating the internal structure of a tool to users—the classic example is "handle means pull, flat plate means push" on a door. At this point, I think (at least some) people have a pretty good understanding of these techniques, and they're spreading over time. But accurate communication of a system's internal structure is only useful if the system's internal structure is itself pretty simple—like a door or a fridge. If I want to, say, write a contract, then I need to interface to the system of contract law; accurately communicating that structure would take a whole book[3], even just to summarize key pieces.

There are lots of systems which are simple enough that accurate communication is the bulk of the problem of interface design—this includes most everyday objects (like fridges), as well as most websites or mobile apps.

But the places where we see expensive industries providing interfaces—like law or software—are usually the cases where the underlying system is more complex. These are cases where the structure of what-humans-want is very different from the system's structure, and translating between the two requires study and practice. Accurate communication of the system's internal structure is not enough to make the problem easy.

In other words: interfaces to complex systems are especially scarce. This economic constraint is very taut, across a number of different areas. We see entire industries—large industries—whose main purpose is to provide non-expert humans with an interface to a particular complex system.

Given that interfaces to complex systems are a scarce resource in general, what other predictions would we make? What else would we expect to be hard/expensive, as a result of interfaces to complex systems being hard/expensive?

AR vs VR

By the standards of software engineering, pretty much anything in the real world is complex. Interfacing to the real world means we don't get to choose the ontology—we can make up a bunch of object types and data structures, but the real world will not consider itself obligated to follow them. The internal structure of computers or programming languages is rarely a perfect match to the structure of the real world.

Interfacing the real world to computers, then, is an area we'd expect to be difficult and expensive.

Augmented reality (AR) is one area where I expect this to be keenly felt, especially compared to VR. I expect AR applications to lag dramatically behind full virtual reality, in terms of both adoption and product quality. I expect AR will mostly be used in stable, controlled environments—e.g. factory floors or escape-room-style on-location games.

Why is interfacing software with the real world hard? Some standard answers:

- The real world is complicated. This is a cop-out answer which doesn't actually explain anything.

- The real world has lots of edge cases. This is also a cop-out, but more subtly; the real world will only seem to be full of edge cases if our program's ontologies don't line up well with reality. The real question: why is it hard to make our ontologies line up well with reality?

Some more interesting answers:

- The real world isn't implemented in Python. To the extent that the real world has a language, that language is math. As software needs to interface more with the real world, it's going to require more math—as we see in data science, for instance—and not all of that math will be easy to black-box and hide behind an API.

- The real world is only partially observable—even with ubiquitous sensors, we can't query anything anytime the way we can with e.g. a database. Explicitly modelling things we can't directly observe will become more important over time, which means more reliance on probability and ML tools (though I don't think black-box methods or "programming by example" will expand beyond niche applications).

- We need enough compute to actually run all that math. In practice, I think this constraint is less taut than it first seems—we should generally be able to perform at least as well as a human without brute-forcing exponentially hard problems. That said, we do still need efficient algorithms.

- The real-world things we are interested in are abstract, high-level objects. At this point, we don't even have the mathematical tools to work with these kinds of fuzzy abstractions.

- We don't directly control the real world. Virtual worlds can be built to satisfy various assumptions by design; the real world can't.

- Combining the previous points: we don't have good ways to represent our models of the real world, or to describe what we want in the real world.

- Software engineers are mostly pretty bad at describing what they want and building ontologies which line up with the real world. These are hard skills to develop, and few programmers explicitly realize that they need to develop them.

Alignment

Continuing the discussion from the previous section, let's take the same problems in a different direction. We said that translating what-humans-want-in-the-real-world into a language usable by computers is hard/expensive. That's basically the AI alignment problem. Does the interfaces-as-scarce-resource view lend any interesting insight there?

First, this view immediately suggests some simple analogues for the AI alignment problem. The "Norman's fridge alignment problem" is one—it's surprisingly difficult to get a fridge to do what we want, when the internal structure of the fridge doesn't match the structure of what we want. Now consider the internal structure of, say, a neural network—how well does that match the structure of what we want? It's not hard to imagine that a neural network would run into a billion-times-more-difficult version of the fridge alignment problem.

Another analogue is the "Ethereum alignment problem": we can code up a smart contract to give monetary rewards for anything our code can recognize. Yet it's still difficult to specify a contract for exactly the things we actually want. This is essentially the AI alignment problem, except we use a market in place of an ML-based predictor/optimizer. One interesting corollary of the analogy: there are already economic incentives to find ways of aligning a generic predictor/optimizer. That's exactly the problem faced by smart contract writers, and by other kinds of contract writers/issuers in the economy. How strong are those incentives? What do the rewards for success look like—are smart contracts only a small part of the economy because the rewards are meager, or because the problems are hard? More discussion of the topic in the next section.

Moving away from analogues of alignment, what about alignment paths/strategies?

I think there's a plausible (though not very probable) path to general artificial intelligence in which:

- We figure out various core theoretical problems, e.g. abstraction, pointers to values, embedded decision theory, ... (See discussion in previous essays. [4, 5, 6])

- The key theoretical insights are incorporated into new programming languages and frameworks

- Programmers can more easily translate what-they-want-in-the-real-world into code, and make/use models of the world which better line up with the structure of reality

- ... and this creates a smooth-ish path of steadily-more-powerful declarative programming tools which eventually leads to full AGI

To be clear, I don't see a complete roadmap yet for this path; the list of theoretical problems is not complete, and a lot of progress would be needed in non-agency mathematical modelling as well. But even if this path isn't smooth or doesn't run all the way to AGI, I definitely see a lot of economic pressure for this sort of thing. We are economically bottlenecked on our ability to describe what we want to computers, and anything which relaxes that bottleneck will be very valuable.

Markets and Contractability

The previous section mentioned the Ethereum alignment problem: we can code up a smart contract to give monetary rewards for anything our code can recognize, yet it's still difficult to specify a contract for exactly the things we actually want. More generally, it's hard to create contracts which specify what we want well enough that they can't be gamed.

(Definitional note: I'm using "contract" here in the broad sense, including pretty much any arrangement for economic transactions— e.g. by eating in a restaurant you implicitly agree to pay the bill later, or boxes in a store implicitly agree to contain what they say on the box. At least in the US, these kinds of contracts are legally binding, and we can sue if they're broken.)

A full discussion of contract specification goes way beyond interfaces—it's basically the whole field of contract theory and mechanism design[7], and encompasses things like adverse selection, signalling, moral hazard, incomplete contracts, and so forth. All of these are techniques and barriers to writing a contract when we *can't* specify exactly what we want. But why can't we specify exactly what we want in the first place? And what happens when we can?

Here's a good example where we can specify exactly what we want: buying gasoline. The product is very standardized, the measures (liters or gallons) are very standardized, so it's very easy to say "I'm buying X liters of type Y gas at time and place Z"—existing standards will fill in the remaining ambiguity. That's a case where the structure of the real world is not too far off from the structure of what-we-want—there's a nice clean interface. Not coincidentally, this product has a very liquid *market*: many buyers/sellers competing over price of a standardized good. Standard efficient-market economics mostly works.

On the other end of the spectrum, here's an example where it's very hard to specify exactly what we want: employing people for intellectual work. It's hard to outsource expertise[8]—often, a non-expert doesn't even know how to tell a job well done from sloppy work. This is a natural consequence of using an expert as an interface to a complicated system. As a result, it's hard to standardize products, and there's not a very liquid market. Rather than efficient markets, we have to fall back on the tools of contract theory and mechanism design—we need ways of verifying that the job is done well without being able to just specify exactly what we want.

In the worst case, the tools of contract theory are insufficient, and we may not be able to form a contract at all. The lemon problem is an example: a seller may have a good used car, and a buyer may want to buy a good used car, but there's no (cheap) way for the seller to prove to the buyer that the car isn't a lemon—so there's no transaction. If we could fully specify everything the buyer wants from the car, and the seller could visibly verify that every box is checked, cheaply and efficiently, then this wouldn't be an issue.

The upshot of all this is that *good interfaces*—tools for translating the structure of the real world into the structure of what-we-want, and vice versa—enable efficient markets. They enable buying and selling with minimal overhead, and they avoid the expense and complexity of contract-theoretic tools.

Create a good interface for specifying what-people-want within some domain, and you're most of the way to creating a market.

Interfaces in Organizations

Accurately communicating what we want is hard. Programmers and product designers are especially familiar with the experience depicted in the cartoon overleaf (next page).

Incentives are a problem sometimes (obviously don't trust ads or salespeople), but even mostly-earnest communicators—customers, project managers, designers, engineers, etc—have a hard time explaining things. In general, people don't understand which aspects are most relevant to other specialists, or often even which aspects are most relevant to themselves. A designer will explain to a programmer the parts which seem most design-relevant; a programmer will pay attention to the parts which seem most programming-relevant.

It's not just that the structure of what-humans-want doesn't match the structure of the real world. It's that the structure of how-human-specialists-see-the-world varies between different specialists. Whenever two specialists in different areas need to convey what-they-want from one to the other, somebody/something has to do the work of translating between structures—in other words, we need an interface.

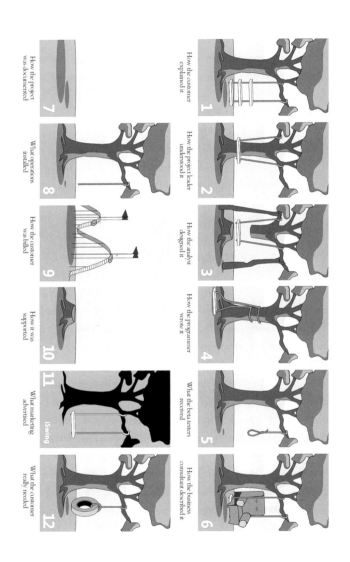

1. How the customer explained it
2. How the project leader understood it
3. How the analyst designed it
4. How the programmer wrote it
5. What the beta testers received
6. How the business consultant described it
7. How the project was documented
8. What operations installed
9. How the customer was billed
10. How it was supported
11. What marketing advertised — iswing
12. What the customer really needed

A particularly poignant example from several years ago: I overheard a designer and an engineer discuss a minor change to a web page. It went something like this:

> Designer: "Ok, I want it just like it was before, but put this part at the top."
>
> Engineer: "Like this?"
>
> Designer: "No, I don't want everything else moved down. Just keep everything else where it was, and put this at the top."
>
> Engineer: "But putting that at the top pushes everything else down."
>
> Designer: "It doesn't need to. Look, just..."

... this went on for about 30 minutes, with steadily increasing frustration on both sides, and steadily increasing thumping noises from my head hitting the desk.

It turned out that the designer's tools built everything from the bottom of the page up, while the engineer's tools built everything from top down. So from the designer's perspective, "put this at the top" did not require moving anything else. But from the engineer's perspective, "put this at the top" meant everything else had to get pushed down.

Somebody/something has to do the translation work. It's a two-sided interface problem.

Handling these sorts of problems is a core function for managers and for anyone deciding how to structure an organization. It may seem silly to need to loop in, say, a project manager for every conversation between a designer and an engineer—but if the project manager's job is to translate, then it can be useful. Remember, the example above was frustrating, but at least both sides *realized* they weren't communicating successfully—if the double illusion of transparency[9] kicks in, problems can crop up without anybody even realizing.

This is why, in large organizations, people who can operate across departments are worth their weight in gold. Interfaces are a scarce resource; people who operate across departments can act as human interfaces, translating model-structures between groups.

A great example of this is the 1986 Goldwater-Nichols Act. It was intended to fix a lack of communication/coordination between branches of the US military. The basic idea was simple: nobody could be promoted to lieutenant or higher without first completing a "joint mission," one in which they worked directly with members of other branches. People capable of serving as interfaces between branches were a scarce resource; Goldwater-Nichols introduced an incentive to create more such people. Before the bill's introduction, top commanders of all branches argued against it; they saw it as congressional meddling. But after the first Iraq war, every one of them testified that it was the best thing to ever happen to the US military.

Summary

The structure of things-humans-want does not always match the structure of the real world, or the structure of how-other-humans-see-the-world. When structures don't match, someone or something needs to serve as an interface, translating between the two.

In simple cases, this is just user interface design—accurately communicating how-the-thing-works to users. But when the system is more complicated—like a computer or a body of law—we usually need human specialists to serve as interfaces. Such people are expensive; interfaces to complicated systems are a scarce resource.

Endnotes

(1) Tania Viera. UX 101: Norman Doors. February, 2020.

(2) Don Norman. The Design of Everyday Things: Revised and Expanded Edition. 5th Nov, 2013.

(3) Charles M. Fox. Working With Contracts: What Law School Doesn't Teach You, 2nd Edition. 1st May, 2008

(4) John S. Wentworth. Abstraction 2020. 6th Dec, 2019.

(5) Abram Demski. Stable Pointers to Value: An Agent Embedded in Its Own Utility Function. 16th Aug, 2017.

(6) Abram Demski and Scott Garrabrant. Decision Theory. 31st Oct, 2018.

(7) Bernard Salanie. The Economics of Contracts: A Primer (2nd Edition). 17th Feb 2017.

(8) John S. Wentworth. What Money Cannot Buy. 1st Feb, 2020.

(9) Eliezer Yudkowsky. The Double Illusion of Transparency. 24th Oct, 2007.

Catherine Olsson

MicroCovid

Editor's note: This post was originally published on August 30 2020, and played an important role in how the LessWrong community assessed personal risk during the pandemic.

Y ou're already familiar with some rules of thumb for avoiding COVID-19 infection: wear a mask, stay six feet apart (or two meters, depending on where you live), and only socialize outdoors. But is it riskier to go to the grocery store, or to ride in a Lyft or Uber? It's tough to make good choices when you don't know how large or small the risks really are.

We, the authors, were really struggling with this. We wanted a better way to make decisions about COVID risk. So we read some papers and crunched some numbers. We spent hours building a model to estimate the COVID risk of various activities. And in this writeup, we'll share our model (and some practical tools!) with you.

We'll show you:

- how we estimate COVID infection risk, in units of "microCOVIDs"

- how risky we think various common activities are

- how you can estimate the COVID risk of your own actions (by hand, or using our handy-dandy calculator[1])

- and, most importantly, how to make decisions that balance living your life with safety and health.

- You're in the target audience of this white paper if you are comfortable with numbers and want to think about how your personal choices affect your chance of getting COVID-19. We are not focusing on society-wide pandemic dynamics, policy responses, or suggestions for public health officials.

We measure the riskiness of interactions in "microCOVIDs"

You might have seen images categorizing COVID risk as "high," "medium," or "low" or rating activities on a riskiness scale from 1 through 9. This is helpful, but personally we found that we had to dig further—into actual numbers—so we could make confident decisions.

Calling an event "high risk" is like categorizing a furniture purchase as "expensive." If I'm buying a rug, and I know it's "expensive," but it would really complete the look of my room, can I afford to splurge this time? Maybe, or maybe not! If the rug is $100, that might be a sensible purchase. But if the rug is $10,000 then I might have difficulty paying for rent and groceries if I buy it!

Similarly: if I've been told that going to gatherings is "high risk" but I really truly miss my friends and there's a picnic coming up I want to attend, should I go? Is this high risk like skiing, or high risk like jumping off a cliff?

We would like to give you a research-based, quantitative framework to answer questions like these.

We can use research to numerically estimate COVID risk

Some people might not realize that it's even possible to measure and numerically quantify the risk of getting COVID. Most sources tend to give non-quantitative advice, such as "the CDC recommends that everyone wear a mask to reduce transmission." This advice is good, but we would like to go even further.

Fortunately, there are now many research papers available about the numerical likelihood of getting COVID from different kinds of interactions. You can search for these studies on Google Scholar and read them yourself. Some of these studies are not peer-reviewed (which is the gold standard for scientific publication), so it's extra important to analyze them carefully. While none of us are public health experts, we have enough academic background to feel comfortable wading into the literature to come up with numerical estimates. We explain more of our reasoning in footnotes and in the Research Sources$_2$ section of our website.

Measuring COVID risk in "microCOVIDs"

So let's get started. To quantify the risk of an individual interaction—say, meeting a friend for coffee—we're going to think in terms of *microCOVIDs* (abbreviated µCoV)★: **a one-in-a-million chance of getting COVID★★**.

★ µ is the standard abbreviation for "micro," the unit prefix meaning "one millionth." For example, one microgram (µg) is one millionth of a gram.
★★ Strictly speaking there is a difference between "getting SARS-CoV-2" (the virus itself) and "getting

1 microCOVID = a one-in-a-million chance of getting COVID

For example, if you live in a region where about 1 in 1,000 people currently has COVID, then you could calculate based on studies of other indoor interactions (as we will explain later in this writeup) that meeting a friend for coffee indoors has about a 1 in 17,000 chance of giving you COVID. Such small numbers are hard to think about, so we can use microCOVIDs instead. Your coffee date would be about 60 microCOVIDs. By the end of this white paper, you will understand how to do these calculations yourself.

One benefit of using microCOVIDs is that you can straightforwardly add up microCOVIDs to estimate your risk over longer periods of time*.

- Here's an example (using some made-up numbers): last week you made two trips to the grocery store (25 microCOVIDs each), went for two masked outdoor walks with friends (1 microCOVID each), and otherwise stayed home alone, so your total risk for that week would be 52 microCOVIDs. You can imagine doing the same calculation over longer time intervals to estimate your chance of getting COVID in a month or even a year of activities.

COVID-19" (the disease caused by the virus). In the rest of this article, no matter what language we use, we are talking about the total chance of getting infected, including if you show no symptoms and are an asymptomatic carrier of the virus. We chose to use "microCOVIDs" (referring to the disease) instead of "microCoV" (referring to the virus) for this article based on reader feedback that it was simpler and easier to understand. But we emphasize that we are not excluding asymptomatic infections from this measurement.

* Technical note—skip if you're not interested in the underlying math! If you've worked with probabilities before, you might worry that adding them together like this is too straightforward to possibly be correct. There's an underlying nonlinearity: while you could accumulate well over a million microCOV-IDs if you do enough risky things, your chance of getting COVID can never be higher than 100%. To properly compute the probability that you remain uninfected despite independent activities A and B, you should calculate "probability not infected via A" * "probability not infected via B". If you'd prefer to add instead of multiplying, then you'll need to take a logarithm somewhere. Thus, to be fully correct, the formula for converting a risk (like 0.01 or 1%) to microCOVIDs should be -1,000,000 * ln(1 - risk). You can use calculus to verify that when the risk is small, this is very well approximated by the simpler 1,000,000 * risk. For values as high as 100,000 microCOVIDs, the error introduced by ignoring the logarithm is still within about 5%. The uncertainty in our other estimates is at least that large, so we think the simplification is reasonable. For calculations involving multiple interactions with substantial risk (any calculation that would result in >10% chance of infection), the calculator switches to multiplying for accuracy.

We use microCOVIDs rather than some other scale factor (milliCOVIDs? nanoCOVIDs?) because they tend to come out as conveniently-sized numbers.

How much is a microCOVID?

This whitepaper was started by a group of 30-something-year-olds in San Francisco who live together in a communal 9-person house and mostly work from home. After much discussion (which we hope to explain later in a future post), the household agreed to aim to keep each housemate's individual risks of getting COVID below **1% per year*** (i.e., about **10,000 microCOVIDs per year**). Important factors in this decision were that nobody in the household regularly interacted with anyone who was at high risk of severe illness from COVID, and that the household collectively cared a lot about doing their part to reduce the spread of the pandemic.

Each person had 2,400 microCOVIDs to spend per year after taking into account how many microCOVIDs would be used up just by living with each other**. With this budget:

An activity that measures this many microCOVIDs...	feels this risky…	… and we could do the activity this often, if we were not doing much else

---

* Technically, what we mean when we say "1% per year" is a 1% annualized risk. That is, if we go 6 months without getting sick, we aren't going to double our chances and bump up to a 2% chance in the following 6 months to even it out. We'll continue at the same 1% annualized risk level.
** We have a detailed write up on how to adjust your budget given the number of people in your household/pod: Using the Risk Tracker with your household/pod.

1 μCoV	almost negligible	dozens of times per week
10 μCoV	moderate risk	a few times per week
100 μCoV	quite substantial risk	once or twice a month
1000 μCoV	borderline reckless	once a year, maybe

Choosing your risk budget

In general, if you are young and healthy, don't regularly visit anyone who is older or has COVID risk factors, and are lucky enough to be able to make voluntary choices about your risk exposure, then we think aiming for 10,000 microCOVIDs per year (corresponding to 1% risk of COVID per year) is a plausible choice.

What we want you to take away from this section is that for people under 40, an activity that is 1 microCOVID is *very low risk*, whereas an activity that is 1,000 microCOVIDs is *very high risk*. Furthermore, any risk of infection that you incur is not just a risk to you, but also a risk to vulnerable people in your community.

Let's now explore how to quantify the risk of various activities in terms of microCOVIDs.

Computing microCOVIDs

In order to calculate the actual risk of an activity in microCOVIDs, we need to combine two numbers:

- **Activity Risk:** the chance that this activity will transmit COVID to you, if the other person currently has COVID.

- **Person Risk:** the chance that the other person currently has COVID. This is based on overall prevalence in your area and their recent behaviors.

For example:

- Let's say you do an activity with someone (like watching a movie indoors) that has an 8% chance of transmitting COVID to you *if* they currently have COVID. We call that an Activity Risk of 8%.

- And let's say that person has a 1% chance of currently being COVID-positive. We call that a Person Risk of 10,000.

    □ Just like for microCOVIDs, if someone has a one-in-a-million chance of having COVID, we'll say their Person Risk is 1.

Then your chance of contracting COVID from that activity-and-person pair is 8% x 10,000 = 800 microCOVIDs (which is the same thing as 0.08%).

In other words, whenever you're deciding to do an activity, ask:

1. How risky is the activity itself?

2. How risky is the person you're doing it with?

We'll think about our actions in terms of how much they "cost" us in microCOVIDs:

$$\text{Cost} = \text{Activity Risk} \times \text{Person Risk}$$

Note that the Activity Risk does *not* factor in the prevalence of COVID in your area. Nor does it take into account the recent behaviors of the person you are interacting with. It is just about the activity itself, specifically how risky it would be if the person currently had COVID.

The Person Risk is the part of the calculation that takes into account the prevalence of COVID in your area, and the other person's recent behaviors, such as whether they have behaved in a lower-risk or higher-risk manner recently.

Let's explore how you can estimate these two numbers (Activity Risk and Person Risk) for an activity you'd like to do.

Activity Risk

Activity Risk is the chance that an activity will transmit COVID to you, *assuming* the other person currently has COVID.

In this section we explain how we estimate Activity Risk for an activity involving one other person. If you just want to compare our risk estimates of specific activities (such as grocery shopping for an hour, or eating in a restaurant), and you are not interested in learning how to do those calculations yourself, you could skip this section and instead explore the example scenarios in the calculator.

Our estimate starts with indoor unmasked conversation

We start by first estimating the risk of interacting with a single COVID-positive person indoors for 1 hour at a normal socializing distance of 3 feet (1 meter) while having a normal-volume conversation.

> Activity Risk of talking to 1 person who has COVID, for 1 hour, indoors, unmasked, at 3 feet (1 meter) = 14%

So if you have a friend over to your house to chat for an hour, and your friend turns out to have COVID, we estimate the chance of you getting COVID from that single interaction as 14%.

How did we come up with this number? It's a rough estimate combining many sources: the Hu et al. train passenger study, the Jimenez Aerosol Transmission Model, Bi et al. which uses contact tracing data, the Chu et al. meta-analysis, and the Cheng et al. prospective study. We have since increased this number by 1.5x based on a study by Davies et al on the increased contagiousness of B.1.1.7., and then again by another 1.5x based on a study of the Delta variant by Allen et al.. For the gory details of how we combine these sources, please see Research Sources.[2]

Think of this as our "reference interaction." We can now use it as a starting point to estimate the risk of other kinds of interactions.

Modifiers: duration, masks, location, distance, volume

Not all interactions are exactly an hour, at a distance of 3 feet (1 meter), etc.

To estimate the Activity Risk of a different interaction (an outdoor picnic, or being in a restaurant), we modify our estimate based on how the interaction in question is different from the "reference interaction" above, based on the following factors:

- duration of interaction

- masks

- location (outdoor vs. indoor)

- distance from each other, and

- volume of conversation.

For example, we might consider having lunch with a friend in the park as interacting for 2 hours (duration), outdoors (location), with someone who is sitting about 6 feet (2 meters) away (distance), without masks because you are eating, talking at a normal volume.

Or we might think of a trip to the grocery store as interacting for 30 minutes (duration), indoors (location), with people who are more than 6 feet (2 meters) away most of the time (distance), who are wearing masks, and who are not talking.

Our estimates for the change in risk based on these modifiers are outlined in the table overleaf.

Modification	Change in COVID risk to me	Citations: Why do we think this?
I'm wearing a surgical mask*	/ 2	Chu et al. meta-analysis (2–3x), Liang et al. meta-analysis (2x), Lai et al. mannequin study (2x)
Other person is wearing a surgical mask	/ 4	Lindsley et al., van der Sande et al., Milton et al., Kumar et al., Davies et al., Fischer et al., O'Kelly et al.
Outdoors	/ 20 or more	Speculative. Suggestive evidence: Qian et al. study of cases in China, Jimenez's Aerosol Transmission Model, lack of surge from BLM protests, anecdotal CO_2 data from protests, zero outdoor outbreaks of any kind, many indoor dining outbreaks, despite both indoor and outdoor dining being open in the US
6+ feet (2+ meters) distance	/ 2	Chu et al. meta-analysis, Hu et al. train passenger study
Each additional 3 feet (1 meter) of distance (up to 12 feet (4 meters))	/ 2	Same as above
Loud talking (shouting, talking over music, singing)	× 5	Jimenez Aerosol Transmission Model
Not talking (such as riding the train)	/ 5	Same as above

* The Calculator1 and Risk Tracker include a more detailed breakdown of different mask types with different multipliers. Our masks research section explains the detailed sources and reasoning for these different types.

If you're taking multiple precautions, multiply the COVID risk reductions together. So if you're wearing a mask *and* they're wearing a mask, then your reduction in COVID risk is $2x \star 4x = 8x$.

What about if the interaction is with more than one other person? We'll get to this later, in the section on Putting it all together. For now, even though it may seem a little silly, we will still imagine there is just one other person (a picnic with one friend, just one other person in the restaurant, etc).

There are plenty of other precautions you can take to reduce your risk that we don't describe here. For more on other precautions, see the Q&A[3].

There is substantial uncertainty in many of these numbers. We've taken uncertainty into account when giving our estimates, so that even if we're off the mark it's unlikely to expose you to much more risk than you're comfortable with. We've also used a slightly conservative prevalence estimate, so that our overall estimates are conservative without distorting the relative risk comparisons. See the discussion of Research Sources[2] for details about the data we based these numbers on.

Example calculations

To calculate the Activity Risk of lunch in the park with your friend, start with 14% (the Activity Risk for our "reference interaction") and apply modifiers as needed: 14% ⋆ 2 (hours) / 20 (outdoors) / 2 (distance of 6-9 feet (2-3 meters)) = 0.7%. You have a **0.7%** chance of getting COVID from this single activity if the other person has COVID. Note that there is no modifier for masks or volume because the reference interaction is already unmasked and at normal volume.

What about indoor dining with that friend? You're there for 2 hours, indoors, at a distance of about 3 feet (1 meter), without masks. Start the same way with 14% and apply modifiers: 14% ⋆ 2 (hours) = 28%. Since the reference interaction is already indoors, at a distance of about 3 feet (1 meter), without masks, and at normal volume, you don't need further modifiers. You have a **28%** chance of getting COVID from your indoor lunch if your friend has COVID.

Compare the risk of getting sick from these interactions: 28% for indoor dining vs. 0.7% for lunch in the park. That's a big difference! Remember, your friend won't necessarily know that they have COVID, and it's very common to be infectious before you show symptoms. And that's with only one person!

Hopefully this puts the risk of indoor gatherings into perspective. To compare the Activity Risk of other activities, such as going grocery shopping or attending a large outdoor party, try our calculator[1] or check out the Q&A[3] for tips and tricks. In the next section, we will look at calculating the risk of activities with multiple people.

Masked, outdoor, distanced interactions are much lower risk

Indoor unmasked interactions are quite risky, but being outdoors and wearing masks both make a *huge* difference.

Masks: We estimate that masks reduce your risk by 8x. This is if *both* people are wearing masks. *Your* mask decreases the risk to *you* by about 2x. And *their* mask decreases risk to *you* by 4x. This assumes a reasonably well-fitting surgical mask[4]. For more protection, there are other types of masks you can wear (addressed in the Q&A[3]). Bandanas, buffs, or other single-layer coverings provide significantly less protection than we estimate here (see Research Sources[2]), so for simplicity we treat them as "no mask", even though we do believe they provide some benefit.

Outdoors: We estimate that being outside reduces your risk by 20x or more because the outdoors is well-ventilated, so small respiratory droplets are less likely to accumulate. With any wind, the risk is even less. We think being outdoors is by far the most valuable thing you can do for your safety, although even that is not a guarantee.

Distance seems to be not quite as beneficial as wearing a mask or being outdoors. We estimate keeping 6 feet (2 meters) apart reduces your risk by 2x, and another 2x for each additional 3 feet (1 meter), up to 12 feet (4 meters). This gives a total risk reduction of:

- 2x if you're 6-9 feet (2-3 meters) away

- 4x if you're 9-12 feet (3-4 meters) away

- 8x if you're >12 feet (>4 meters) away

Catherine Olsson

If you're outdoors *and* 20 feet (7 meters) away from a person, you can probably ignore the risk from them.

Volume of conversation also matters. If the other person isn't talking, we estimate that reduces the risk to you by about 5x, because they are not expelling as many respiratory droplets. This actually makes some activities where people don't talk much, such as taking public transportation, safer than they would otherwise be. On the other hand, we estimate that loud talking, shouting, or singing *increases* the risk by about 5x (as compared to a conversation at normal volume) because more respiratory droplets are exhaled and expelled when you are speaking or breathing forcefully.

Curious how we got these numbers? Again, check out the Research Sources[2]!

Household members and spouses/partners are estimated differently

We do the calculation differently for household members and spouses/partners because you're likely to interact with them on a recurring basis. We estimate a single, fixed Activity Risk for one week of living in the same household as someone who is COVID-positive.

Activity Risk of living with 1 household member, who
has COVID, for 1 week = 40%

Activity Risk of living with 1 spouse/partner, who
has COVID, for 1 week = 60%

These numbers clearly show that if your housemate gets COVID, it is *not* inevitable that you will get COVID too! Even if your spouse or partner (who you are likely to share a bed with) gets COVID, your chance of getting it is still only about 60%.

You might ask: why isn't the risk of getting COVID from someone in your house higher? Why is the estimate of household member risk (40%) only as bad as about 3 hours of hanging out indoors with a friend (at 14% per hour)? We don't really know why this is, but we do know that over the last year and a half, studies continued to find transmission rates within a household well below 100%. Some hypotheses include:

- Individuals have orders of magnitude differences in the amount of aerosols they produce, this could lead to some people just never becoming contagious.

- The period of maximum contagiousness may be as short as 12 hours. If housemates/spouses happen to not interact with each other in this window, the chance of infection drops.

- Housemates/partners may isolate from each other upon noticing symptoms, which reduces the chance of transmission.

- The hourly rate of transmission is likely non-linear, i.e. 3 hours in a row with someone is likely less risky than 3x the risk of 1 hour.

The original household member estimate comes directly from Curmei et al. meta-analysis. The partner estimate is very speculative, based on adjusting Curmei et al. using a datapoint from Li et al.. We increased the household transmission rate for delta based on Allen et al.. We scaled the partner transmission rate based on the same study. See Research Sources[2] for slightly more detail and to learn about the scientific research supporting our estimates.

How likely is it that the other person has COVID?

Now we understand Activity Risk, or how your chance of getting the virus changes based on the activity you're doing. But Activity Risk *assumes* the other person is COVID-positive. What are the actual chances that whoever you're interacting with has COVID? Let's look at Person Risk to understand that.

Person Risk

Person Risk is the chance that the other person currently has COVID. This is based on overall prevalence in your area and their recent behaviors.

So you've decided to meet a friend for lunch. You know the Activity Risk is 14% per hour (for an indoor unmasked lunch) and much less if you MODify[5] your hangout. But the Activity Risk *assumes* that they currently have COVID.

What's the chance that your friend actually has COVID? They aren't coughing and they feel totally fine. Can you conclude they aren't infected? Unfortunately, no. Roughly 55% of COVID transmissions[6] happen when the person has *no symptoms*.*

---

* Note that this figure includes both presymptomatic transmissions (where the person transmitting COVID will eventually show symptoms, usually within a few days, but hasn't yet) and asymptomatic transmissions (where the person transmitting will never show symptoms). Catching COVID from some-one presymptomatic is much more common: this accounts for about 50% of all transmissions, as opposed to asymptomatic transmissions which account for only about 5%. The COVID discourse tends to muddy this fact somewhat. Asymptomatic infections are inherently harder to measure (because you probably won't get tested if you don't show symptoms), and there are indeed plenty of them. However, most of them don't infect anyone else.

Not all diseases work this way. For example, Ebola is only contagious when the person is already exhibiting symptoms. However, COVID is a different disease, and one of its defining features is that it has a high rate of transmission from people *who don't yet have symptoms*.

This means that the chance someone has COVID (which we're calling "Person Risk") depends on their actions and choices in the past 10 days or so, not just whether they're actively showing symptoms.

We use three different methods of guessing someone's chance of having COVID.

- The **Basic Method** is to just assume the person is "average" for their region. The chance your friend has COVID is the chance that *anyone* in your geographic area has COVID.

- The **Advanced Method** is to add up the risk of each individual activity that person has done recently.

You do not need to understand exactly how these methods work to use the Calculator, but if you want to create your own custom estimates for specific people in your life then we strongly recommend learning to use the Advanced Method and the associated risk tracking tool[4].

Skip ahead and takeaways

If you would like to skip ahead, please first read the following takeaways that we think are the most important things conveyed in the next few sections:

- **The chance someone has COVID is very different in different geographic regions.**

  - The very same activity that is fairly safe where I live might be fairly dangerous where my parents live, because the risk that people have COVID there is higher.

If you would like to understand how we use the basic and advanced methods to calculate Person Risk, read on.

Skip ahead to Putting it all together, or read on about the Basic Method for more detail.

The Basic Method of calculating Person Risk is the regional average

As we know, prevalence varies widely across different geographic locations. For example, at the time of writing, Sydney has much lower rates of COVID than San Francisco. So the Person Risk from your friend in Sydney will be much lower than the risk from your friend in San Francisco.

The **Basic Method** is to just assume that a person is "average" for their region. The chance your friend has COVID is the chance that *anyone* in their geographic area has COVID.

How we estimate the regional average

To estimate the chance that a random resident in your area has COVID, you need to figure out the number of **new infections last**

week in your area. This is because a typical person is infectious for about a one-week period.★

We will give an overview of the steps, then explain the steps in more detail.

1. Start with the number of new reported cases in your region last week. The calculator does this automatically for you, or you can look up these numbers manually by Googling.

However, this is just a start. You cannot use this number directly because it underestimates how many people are actually sick. You need to take into account two important factors.

2. The first factor is **underreporting**. Many people with COVID won't ever get counted in the official statistics. They might not think their symptoms are anything unusual, so they don't get tested. Or they might not be able to access testing.★★

3. The second factor is **delay**. There's a delay of 1-2 weeks between when someone becomes infected and when their positive test result comes back. The true number of confirmed cases who were sick *last* week isn't known yet, and won't be known until those tests come back *next* week. If cases are rising, last week's statistics will be too low.

The calculator can look up new reported cases automatically, and takes these adjustments into account as well.

★ The most-infectious period starts a couple days after infection, but the day-to-day noise in new case numbers is enough that "0-7 days ago" and "2-9 days ago" are unlikely to be meaningfully different. See Research Sources for more about the infectious period.

★★ As an example, New York City in March–April 2020 was completely overwhelmed by COVID, with widespread reports that even people with obvious and severe symptoms were unable to receive a test. We'll look specifically at the five boroughs plus Westchester, Nassau, and Suffolk counties, an area containing 12.2 million residents. A survey for COVID antibodies in these counties performed between April 25–May 6 found that 23% of people had previously been infected, but according to the Johns Hopkins dashboard only 263,900 cases (2.2% of the area's population) had been officially recorded by May 1.

The chance someone has COVID is very different in different geographic regions.

While we were working on this writeup, in July 2020, we calculated the Person Risk (Basic Method) in San Francisco as about 5107-in-a-million, and about 84-in-a-million in Sydney.

This means that the risk of doing a specific activity in San Francisco that month was about 60 times higher than doing the same activity in Sydney.

Inviting **one** random person over for coffee (indoors, unmasked, undistanced) in San Francisco would've been about as risky as inviting **60** random Sydney residents to your home!

There is not just one answer for "How risky is it to invite one person over for coffee?" It depends on where they live and how widespread COVID is there.

Detailed steps for Basic Method

To learn how to do these steps manually, or to understand how the calculator does it, read the rest of this page.

Step one: Look up reported cases

To estimate the prevalence of COVID where you live, start by looking up the number of reported cases last week in your region.

- Make sure to look up *new* cases, not *total* cases.

- Make sure to get statistics for a *week*, not a *day*.

You decide how to define your region. This might be based on the county where you live, or you might want to include multiple counties if you live in a major metropolitan area. If data is limited, you might have to use your entire state.

If you live in the US, you can use the CovidEstim[7] website. This gives *daily* new reported cases per 100,000 people. To get a week's worth of cases, you'll need to calculate: daily new reported cases per 100,000 people * 7 days.* will then use 100,000 as the population.

Step two: Underreporting factor

Many people with COVID won't ever get counted in the official statistics. The official statistics are **underreporting** the real number of new infections.

You can use the *positive test rate* (the percentage of tests that come back COVID-positive) as some evidence about how many infections are being caught by testing. Ideally, the positive test rate should be very low, indicating that contact tracing is working to find all contacts of an infected person, and that testing is available for each contact. If a high percentage of tests are coming back positive, then there are probably a lot *more* infected people out there than the testing data shows.

If you live in the US, you can look up the positive test rate in your state at CovidActNow[8].

We use the correction factor proposed by COVID-19 Projections[9]:

---

* It's not very obvious from their website, but CovidActNow's daily numbers are smoothed by taking the average over the past 7 days. Thus, this calculation will correctly compute the number of cases last week, not just 7 times the number of cases yesterday. You might find that other sources of data do this as well.

prevalance_ratio = 1250 / (day_i + 25) * positive_test_rate ** 0.5 + 2

true_infections = prevalance_ratio * reported_infections

where day_i = number of days since 2020-02-12

More details are available in Research Sources or on COVID-19 Projection's website.

Step three: Delay factor

Since test results take about one week to come back on average, the number of *new reported cases* in your region last week really represents the number of *new positive test results* in your region *the week before that*. The results are **delayed**.

If cases are flat or falling, it's fine to use this number as is.

If cases are rising, then we need to estimate the increase by comparing last week's reported case numbers to the week before that. For example, if last week there were 120 reported cases, and the previous week there were 80 reported cases, then the weekly increase is 120 / 80 = 1.5. We would use 1.5x as our delay factor. To avoid over-extrapolating from a single superspreader event in an otherwise low-prevalence area, we have capped the delay factor at 2x.

- In the calculator this would be displayed as a 50% increase in cases from last week to this week.

Step four: Estimate number of new infections last week

Use this equation to combine the previous three steps to estimate the regional prevalence of COVID in your area:

$$\text{New Infections Last Week} = \text{Reported Cases} \times$$
$$\text{Underreporting Factor} \times \text{Delay Factor}$$

Step five: Divide by population to get a final estimate

From there, calculate the basic Person Risk by comparing the new infections last week with the overall population in your region.

$$\text{Person Risk (Basic)} = \text{New Infections Last Week} / \text{Population In Millions}$$

Example Sydney and San Francisco calculations

Here are two examples:

Sydney in July 2020 (lower prevalence)

- Step 1: As of July 26, 2020, the state of New South Wales in Australia (where Sydney is located) had 81 reported cases in the last week, and a population of around 7.5 million.

- Step 2: The week before that, there were 62 reported cases. 81 / 62 = 1.3 so we'll use a 1.3x delay factor, i.e. a 30% increase in cases from last week to this week.

- Step 3: The percentage of positive COVID tests is extremely low: 81 cases / 135,089 tests = 0.05% so we'll use our minimum 6x underreporting factor.*

---

* With this low of a positive test rate, an even lower underreporting factor is quite plausible, but we don't have enough data to estimate just how low we should go.

- Step 4: Therefore, 81 reported cases ★ 1.3 ★ 6 = 632 new infections last week.

- Step 5: So the Person Risk (the chance that a random resident in New South Wales has COVID) is 632 infections / 7,500,000 people = 0.000084 or 0.0084%.

  - An easier way to talk about this tiny number is to multiply it by a million: 0.000084 ★ 1,000,000 = 84.

  - This is the same as if we had just divided by 7.5 (the population in *millions*).

So if all you knew about a person is that they lived in New South Wales in July 2020, their Person Risk at the time would've been **84**, which means there's a **84-in-a-million** chance that they had COVID (in that particular week).

San Francisco in July 2020 (higher prevalence)

Compare this with San Francisco County in California, which had 749 new reported cases during that same week, and a population of 0.88 million.★ Cases at that time were declining, so we won't use a delay factor. The positive test rate was 4.3%, so we'll use a 6x underreporting factor. Therefore, 749 reported cases ★ 6 = 4494 new infections last week. To get the Person Risk, divide by the population (in millions): 4494 infections / 0.88 million people = 5107.★★ So a

---

★ Tip: if your data source lists a "7-day moving average" of cases on a certain day, the number of cases in the preceding week is just 7 times that.
★★ This seems high to us: a 5107-in-a-million chance over a week-long period of getting COVID from being an average SF resident implies the average SF resident has a 23% annualized chance of getting COVID. That seems pretty bad. We really hope we're wrong somewhere and the real number is lower; perhaps we don't need as high as a 6x underreporting factor anymore?

resident of San Francisco had a Person Risk of **5107**, or a **5107-in-a-million** chance of currently having COVID (for this particular week).

Comparing the above examples

5107-in-a-million (in San Francisco) is about 60 times higher than 84-in-a-million (in Sydney). So the average Person Risk in San Francisco is 60x as high as in Sydney!

The Advanced Method makes a list of the person's recent behavior

To get a more accurate estimate for Person Risk, we can actually add up the risk (in microCOVIDs) of their recent behavior. Remember, a single microCOVID represents a one-in-a-million chance of getting COVID.

The **Advanced Method** is to add up the risk of each individual activity that person has done recently.

The Risk Tracker[4] is a tool that can help you add up activities in the Advanced Method.

Just like you can calculate this for each of your actions, you can also calculate it for your friend's actions, using the same formula:

Cost = Activity Risk × Person Risk

We can do this by looking at all of their activities between 2–9 days ago* and determining the risk of each individual activity. Or if they do the same things every week, what does their typical week look like?

This is an advanced method because it requires asking about and calculating the risk of each of your friend's recent or typical errands, hangouts, and other activities. And you might have to ask about your friend's contacts too!

Add up the person's socializing, errands, and work

The advanced method hinges on getting an accurate picture of all of your contacts' activities and risks. This requires examining their lives in more scrutiny than you may be used to in normal times. To help, we've developed a list of questions[10] to ensure you are thorough in assessing their risk.

We think about risk in three categories: socializing, errands, and work. To calculate total Person Risk using the advanced method, you can add these three categories together, as follows:

Person Risk (Advanced) = Socializing + Errands + Work

Note that this formula uses addition, whereas everything else we've done until now has been multiplication.

---

* The 2-9 day window is an approximation for people who keep relatively constant schedules or maintain a similar level of risky behaviors week over week (for instance, by using microCOVID to track their own activities). If this is not a good description of the person's behavior (e.g. they recently took a flight, went to a party or indoor restaurant, or had contact with someone with COVID), it is necessary to count up all their activities from the last 2-23 days (3 weeks). Events past 5 days have diminishing effects on their riskiness, which makes this method difficult to do by hand. The Risk Tracker handles this calculation for us. For details on how this is derived, see Research Sources.

For socializing, just estimate each social activity in microCOVIDs (using "Cost = Activity Risk ⊠ Person Risk") and add them together. This is the place to count the exposure from all their household members as well.

Errands include grocery shopping, transit, and other public settings. These can be harder to estimate individually; we have some guidelines in the Q&A₃.

Work is modeled just like the above socializing and errands, and you would ask similar kinds of questions: how many people is this person sharing indoor air space with? For how many hours per week? What is their risk profile like?

Though you can do Advanced Method calculations on your own, the Risk Tracker was designed for that very purpose. It is a helpful tool for both individuals and households/pods who want to manage their risk.

The best way to understand how to apply the Advanced Method is through an example. See the next section for a detailed example.

Comparing Person Risk methods with an example

Let's work through a quick example to compare the different approaches for estimating Person Risk.

Reasonable Rosie lives with one roommate in San Francisco and works from home. Rosie grocery shops twice a week in a surgical mask. Nobody else visits Rosie's apartment, and she doesn't hang out with anyone else indoors. She went on 5 separate 1.5 hour masked, outdoor, regular distance (3-feet (1 meter) apart) walks with friends over the past ten days. For simplicity, we'll assume her roommate does the exact same set of activities that she does.

You're planning to hang out with Rosie and want to know her Person Risk, so you can know what precautions to take. You calculate:

- Basic method: **5106** Person Risk.

  - Because we estimate the San Francisco prevalence of COVID infection (at the time of writing) as 5106-in-a-million. This would change if prevalence changed.

- Advanced method: **217** Person Risk

  - Remember, here you're calculating **Rosie's own** risk of getting COVID from **her** activities, in microCOVIDs, which you can then use in calculating **your** risk of getting COVID from her.

  - Each walk starts with a 14% Activity Risk (for one-time contact per hour) times 1.5 hours, and then gets a decrease of 2x for Rosie's mask, 4x for her friend's mask, and 20x for being outdoors. Since she stays 3 feet (1 meter) apart from friends on these walks, there is no additional reduction for distance. We'll treat the friends as average residents (using the 5106 Person Risk from the Basic Method above). Five walks in the past ten days adds up to 0.14/hr × 1.5hr × 5 × 5106 × ($\frac{1}{2}$) × ($\frac{1}{4}$) × ($\frac{1}{20}$) = 34 microCOVIDs.

  - Rosie also goes to the grocery store twice a week. We estimate this as spending 2 hours per week, about six feet (two meters) away (2x) from 5 random people at a time (each with 5106

Person Risk using the Basic Method), wearing a surgical mask (2x). Let's assume the other people in the store are wearing thick and snug cloth masks (3x, not as protective as surgical masks), but that people are not talking (5x decrease). Rosie's grocery shopping adds up to $5106 \times 0.14/\text{hr} \times 2\text{hr} \times 5\times (\frac{1}{2}) \times (\frac{1}{3}) \times (1/5) = 238$ microCOVIDs.

□ So Rosie's errands plus her walks gives her a risk of $238 + 34 = 272$ microCOVIDs (or 272-in-a-million chance of catching COVID).

□ If Rosie's roommate does the same things (two hours of grocery shopping and five walks with friends per week), then Rosie's roommate's risk of getting COVID, in microCOVIDs, *due to sources other than Rosie*, is the same: 272. Multiply this by the 40% Activity Risk of being a roommate and you learn that Rosie's roommate poses a risk to Rosie of $0.40 \times 272 = 109$ microCOVIDs.*

□ So the total COVID risk for Rosie, based on her behaviors, is $238 + 34 + 109 = 381$ microCOVIDs. Now you can use this number as the "Person Risk" when you're calculating your own chance of getting COVID from Rosie.

One thing you will notice is that when we re-compute Rosie's Person Risk via the advanced method, we get substantially smaller numbers. This is because the Basic method assumes Rosie is about average, which is not true. In fact, she is being about ten times more cautious than the average person in her geographic area. The more you know

---

* If the people in your household/pod have any significant exposure to the outside world (including groceries, essential work, etc.) then you will need to include your own contact with your housemates (or others in your pod) in your estimate of how many microCOVIDs of exposure you have incurred, because those people's Activity Risk is not zero. The fact that they are in your pod does not change the fact that everything they have done in the past 10 days poses a risk to you. See our household/pod documentation for more info on managing risk in that setting.

about a person's behavior, the more accurate your estimate can be. In some cases it might go up, in other cases it might go down.

With a total COVID risk of 381 microCOVIDs, Rosie is being much more cautious than average!* It's also possible we're still overestimating her risk, even using the Advanced Method. For example, if her friends are similar to her, then they are probably more cautious than average as well, which would reduce her COVID risk from socializing.

In our calculator we've provided some Person Risk Profiles that were made using the Advanced Method. You can use them as a starting point to create your own calculations.

Now that we've looked at Person Risk, we can combine it with Activity Risk to get the cost in microCOVIDs of a given activity. Hooray, you made it!

Putting it all together

We can now multiply Activity Risk by Person Risk to get the microCOVID cost of a given interaction.

$$Cost = Activity\ Risk \times Person\ Risk$$

---

* If Reasonable Rosie keeps up this rate of 381 microCOVIDs per week, she'll incur about 20,000 microCOVIDs per year, which implies about a 2% chance of getting COVID during that year. This is much lower than the average American!

Multiple-person interactions

So far we have assumed you are interacting with just one other person (a picnic with one friend, just one other person in the restaurant, etc).

If you are interacting with multiple people (lunch with *two* friends; being near *five* people at a time in a grocery store), you can add the microCOVID costs together, i.e., multiply by the number of people.

> Cost = Activity Risk × Person Risk for one person ×
> Number of people

In the calculator we display the Person Risk for *each* person.

An example of combining Activity Risk and Person Risk to get a total Cost

Let's say you would like to spend an afternoon catching up with Reasonable Rosie (from an earlier example), whose Person Risk is 381 using the Advanced Method. An indoors meetup has a 14% Activity Risk per hour, so it costs you 14% per hour × 2 hours × 381 Person Risk = **107 microCOVIDs**.

> 107 microCOVIDs = 14% per hour (Activity Risk) × 2 hr ×
> 381 (Person Risk)

If you both wear surgical masks, it costs you 8x less: only **13 microCOVIDs**. And if you hang out outside instead of inside, it costs you an *additional* 20x less, for just 0.7 microCOVIDs (**less than 1 microCOVID!**)

$$0.7 \text{ microCOVIDs} = 14\% \text{ per hour} \times 2 \text{ hr} \times (\tfrac{1}{8} \text{ masks}) \times$$
$$(\tfrac{1}{20} \text{ outdoors}) \times 381 \text{ (Person Risk)}$$

Should you do these activities? It depends on how important you believe it is to avoid COVID (for your own health, and to protect others), and how important seeing Rosie is to you!

- If you're aiming for 1% risk of COVID per year (833 microCOVIDs per month), an indoor unmasked hangout with Reasonable Rosie is something you can do multiple times per month, and you can treat the outdoor masked hangout as totally "free."

- However, if you're aiming for 0.1% risk per year (83 microCOVIDs per month), *one* unmasked indoor hangout with Reasonable Rosie is more risk than you'd be willing to spend in an *entire month*. To spend your microCOVIDs more efficiently, you'll want to use protective measures like wearing a mask or only hanging out outdoors. Unless, of course, Reasonable Rosie is the only person you want to see all month and you don't need to do groceries.

- And if you're highly vulnerable and aiming for 0.01% risk per year (8.3 microCOVIDs per month), the outdoor mask walk is something you can afford to do, but you *cannot* hang out indoors with Reasonable Rosie *even once* without jeopardizing a large fraction of your budget for the entire year.

Now that you have seen the whole process end-to-end and several example numbers, it might be a good time to revisit "How much is a microCOVID?".

Remember that Reasonable Rosie is a specific example person, from a specific example place and time. Her risk of having COVID depends on her recent hypothetical behaviors. If you're hanging out with someone at a different place or time, the Activity Risk would be the same, but the Person Risk is likely to be very different, and so the overall Cost would be very different.

We hope our mindset towards COVID risk modeling helps you feel less trapped and more free to live a safe(r) COVID life.

Endnotes

(1) https://www.microcovid.org/calculator

(2) https://www.microcovid.org/paper/all#14-research-sources

(3) https://www.microcovid.org/paper/all#13-q-and-a

(4) A. C. K. Lai,* C. K. M. Poon, and A. C. T. Cheung. Effectiveness of facemasks to reduce exposure hazards for airborne infections among general populations. 2012.

(5) https://www.microcovid.org/paper/all#mod-hang-outs-masked-outdoors-distance

(6) Ferretti et al. Quantifying SARS-CoV-2 transmission suggests epidemic control with digital contact tracing. 31st Mar 2020.

(7) https://covidestim.org/

(8) https://covidactnow.org/

(9) https://covid19-projections.com/estimating-true-infections-revis-ited/

(10) https://www.microcovid.org/questions

Jacob Falkovich

Seeing the Smoke

Originally published on February 28 2020.

Author's Note: While COVID-19 being a major pandemic outside China was merely a possibility in the early weeks of 2020, it was understandable that a few informed people began prepping while most ignored it. But the second half of February was much stranger: as the pandemic turned from possible to inevitable given the data on worldwide exponential spread, public response and preparation remained mostly frozen. For a couple of weeks, many people who were most sane in their anticipation of COVID-19 were questioning their sanity given the overwhelming non-response of the public around — this post was written in those two weeks.

COVID-19 could be pretty bad for you. It could affect your travel plans as countries impose quarantines and close off borders. It could affect you materially as supply chains are disrupted and stock markets are falling. Even worse: you could get sick and suffer acute respiratory symptoms. Worse than that: someone you care about may die, likely an elderly relative.

But the worst thing that could happen is that you're seen doing something about the coronavirus before you're given permission to.

I'll defend this statement in a minute, but first of all: I am now giving you permission to do something about COVID-19. You have permission to read up on the symptoms of the disease and how it spreads. Educate yourself on the best ways to avoid it. Stock up on obvious essentials such as food, water, soap, and medicine, as well as less obvious things[1] like oxygen saturation monitors so you know if you need emergency care once you're sick. You should decide ahead of time what your triggers are for changing your routines or turtling up at home.

In fact, you should go do all those things before reading the rest of the post. I am not going to provide any more factual justifications for preparing. If you've been following the news and doing the research, you can decide for yourself. And if instead of factual justifications you've been following the cues of people around you to decide when it's *socially acceptable* to prep for a pandemic, then all you need to know is that I've already put my reputation on the line[2] as a corona prepper.

Instead this post is about the strange fact that most people need social approval to prepare for a widely reported pandemic.

Smoke Signals

As Eliezer reminded us[3], most people sitting alone in a room will quickly get out if it starts filling up with smoke. But if two other people in the room seem unperturbed, almost everyone will stay put. That is the result of a famous experiment from the 1960s[4] and its replications—people will sit and nervously look around at their peers for 20 minutes even as thick smoke starts obscuring their vision.

The coronavirus was identified on January 7th and spread outside China by the 13th. The American media ran some stories about how you should worry more about the seasonal flu. The markets didn't budge. Rationalist Twitter started tweeting excitedly about r0 and supply chains.

Over the next two weeks, Chinese COVID cases kept climbing at 60%/day reaching 17,000 by February 2nd. Cases were confirmed in Europe and the US. The WHO declared a global emergency. The former FDA commissioner explained[5] why a law technicality[6] made it illegal for US hospitals to test people for coronavirus, implying that we would have no idea how many Americans have contracted the disease. Everyone mostly ignored him including all major media publications, and equity markets hit an all-time high. By this point several Rationalists in Silicon Valley and elsewhere started seriously prepping for a pandemic and canceling large social gatherings.

On the 13th, Vox published a story[7] mocking people in Silicon Valley for worrying about COVID-19. The article contained multiple factual mistakes about the virus and the opinions of public health experts.

On February 17th, Eliezer asked how markets should react[8] to an obvious looming pandemic. Most people agreed that the markets should freak out and weren't. Most people decided to trust the markets over their own judgment. As an avowed efficient marketeer[9] who hasn't made an active stock trade in a decade, I started at that Tweet for a long time. I stared at it some more. Then I went ahead and sold 10% of the stocks I owned and started buying respirators and beans.

By the 21st, the pandemic and its concomitant shortages hit everywhere from Iran to Italy while in the US thousands of people were asked to self-quarantine[10]. Most elected officials in the US seemed utterly unaware that anything was happening. CNN ran a front page story about the real enemies being racism and the seasonal flu[11].

Finally, the narrative couldn't contain the sheer volume of disconfirming evidence. The stock market tumbled 10%. The Washington Post squeezed out one more story about racism[12] before confirming that the virus is spreading among Americans with no links to Wuhan[13] and that's scary. Trump decided to throw his vice president[14] under the coronavirus bus, finally admitting that it's a thing that the government is aware of.

And Rationalist Twitter asked[15]: what the fuck is wrong with everyone who is not on Rationalist Twitter?

Cognitive Reflection

Before Rationality gained a capital letter and a community, a psychologist developed a simple test[16] to identify people who can override an intuitive and wrong answer with a reflective and correct one.

One of the questions is:

In a lake, there is a patch of lily pads. Every day, the patch doubles in size. If it takes 48 days for the patch to cover the entire lake, how long would it take for the patch to cover half of the lake?

Exponential growth is hard for people to grasp. Most people answer "24" to the above question, or something random like "35". It's counterintuitive to people that the lily pads could be barely noticeable on day 44 and yet completely cover the lake on day 48.

Here's another question, see if you can get it:

In an interconnected world, cases of a disease outside the country of origin are doubling every 5 days. The pace is slightly accelerating since it's easier to contain a hundred sick people than it is to contain thousands. How much of a moron do you have to be as a journalist to quote statistics about the yearly toll of seasonal flu given a month of exponential global growth of a disease with 20 times the mortality rate[17]?

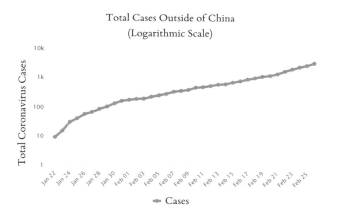

Total Cases Outside of China
(Logarithmic Scale)

Social Reality Strikes Again

Human intuition is bad at dealing with exponential growth but it's very good at one thing: not looking weird in front of your peers. It's so good at this, in fact, that the desire to not look weird will override most incentives.

Journalists would rather miss out on the biggest story of the decade than stick their neck out with an alarmist article. Traders would rather miss out on billions of dollars of profits[18]. People would rather get sick than do something that isn't socially sanctioned.

Even today (2/26/2020), most people I've spoken to refuse to do minimal prep for what could be the worst pandemic in a century. It costs $100 to stock up your house with a month's worth of dry food and disinfectant wipes (respirators, however, are now sold out or going for 4x the price). People keep waiting for the government to do something, even though the government has proven its incompetence in this area several times over.

I think I would replace the Cognitive Reflection Test with a single question: would you eat a handful of coffee beans[19] if someone told you it was worth trying? Or in other words: do you understand that social reality can diverge from physical reality, the reality of coffee beans and viruses and diseases?

Social thinking is quite sufficient for most people in usual times. But this is an unusual time.

Seeing the Smoke

The goal of this article isn't to get all my readers to freak out about the virus. Aside from selling the equities, all the prep I've done was to stock a month of necessities so I can work from home and to hold off on booking flights for a trip I had planned for April.

The goal of this post is twofold. First, if you're the sort of person who will keep sitting in a smoke-filled room until someone else gets up, I'm here to be that someone for you. If you're a regular reader of Putanumonit[20] you probably respect my judgment and you know that I'm not particularly prone to getting sucked into panics and trends.

And second, if you watched that video thinking that you would obviously jump out of the room at the first hint of smoke, ask yourself how much research and preparation you've done for COVID-19 given the information available. If the answer is "little to none", consider whether that is rational or *rationalizing*.

I could wait to write this post two months from now when it's clear how big of an outbreak occurs in the US. I'm not an expert on viral diseases, global supply chains, or prepping. I don't have special information or connections. My only differentiation is that I care a bit less than others about appearing weird or foolish, and I trust a bit more in my own judgment

Seeing the smoke and reacting is a learnable skill, and I'm going to give credit to Rationality for teaching it[21]. I think COVID-19 is the best exam for Rationalists doing much better than "common sense" since Bitcoin. So instead of waiting two months, I'm submitting my answer for reality to grade. I think I'm seeing smoke.

Endnotes

(1) https://theprepared.com/wuhan-coronavirus/

(2) Jakeup. 24th Feb 2020 on Twitter.

(3) https://intelligence.org/2017/10/13/fire-alarm/

(4) http://www.weirduniverse.net/blog/comments/the_smoke_filled_room

(5) Scott Gottlieb, MD. 2nd Feb 2020 on Twitter.

(6) Eddie, Son of Richard. 24th Feb 2020 on Twitter.

(7) https://www.vox.com/recode/2020/2/13/21128209/coronavirus-fears-contagion-how-infection-spreads

(8) Eliezer Yudkowsky. 17th Feb 2020 on Twitter.

(9) https://putanumonit.com/2017/02/10/get-rich-slowly/

(10) https://www.pressdemocrat.com/article/news/california-tells-7600-people-to-self-quarantine-because-of-coronavirus/

(11) https://edition.cnn.com/2020/02/20/us/coronavirus-racist-attacks-against-asian-americans/

(12) https://www.washingtonpost.com/health/2020/02/25/shen-yun-coronavirus-fears-utah/

(13) https://www.washingtonpost.com/health/northern-californian-tests-positive-for-coronavirus-in-first-us-case-with-no-link-to-foreign-

*travel/2020/02/26/b2088840-58fb-11ea-9000-f3cffee23036_story.
html*

*(14) https://thehill.com/policy/healthcare/484858-trump-names-
pence-to-lead-coronavirus-response*

(15) William Eden. 26th Feb 2020 on Twitter.

(16) https://sjdm.org/dmidi/Cognitive_Reflection_Test.html

*(17) https://www.worldometers.info/coronavirus/coronavi-
rus-death-rate*

*(18) https://putanumonit.com/2016/11/16/flip-flops-part-1-of-
%E2%88%9E/*

*(19) https://putanumonit.com/2019/10/16/polyamory-is-ration-
al/#social*

(20) https://putanumonit.com/

*(21) https://putanumonit.com/2019/12/08/rationalist-self-improve-
ment/*

alkjash

Pain is not the unit of effort

(Content warning: self-harm, parts of this post may be actively counterproductive for readers with certain mental illnesses or idiosyncrasies.)

What doesn't kill you makes you stronger. ~ Kelly Clarkson.

No pain, no gain. ~ Exercise motto.

The more bitterness you swallow, the higher you'll go. ~ Chinese proverb.

I noticed recently that, at least in my social bubble, *pain is the unit of effort*. In other words, how hard you are trying is explicitly measured by how much suffering you put yourself through. In this post, I will share some anecdotes of how damaging and pervasive this belief is, and propose some counterbalancing ideas that might help rectify this problem.

I. Anecdotes

1. As a child, I spent most of my evenings studying mathematics under some amount of supervision from my mother. While studying, if I expressed discomfort or fatigue, my mother would bring me a snack or drink and tell me to stretch or take a break. I think she took it as a sign that I was trying my best. If on the other hand I was smiling or joyful for extended periods of time, she took that as a sign that I had effort to spare and increased the hours I was supposed to study each day. To this day there's a gremlin on my shoulder that whispers, "If you're happy, you're not trying your best."

2. A close friend who played sports in school reports that training can be *harrowing*. He told me that players who fell behind the pack during daily jogs would be singled out and publicly humiliated. One time the coach screamed at my friend for falling behind the asthmatic boy who was alternating between running and using his inhaler. Another time, my friend internalized "no pain, no gain" to the point of losing his toenails.

3. In high school and college, I was surrounded by overachievers constantly making (what seemed to me) incomprehensibly bad life choices. My classmates would sign up for eight classes per semester when the recommended number is five, jigsaw extracurricular activities into their calendar like a dynamic programming knapsack-solver, and then proceed to have loud public complaining contests about which libraries are most comfortable to study at past 2am and how many pages they have left to write for the essay due in three hours. Only later did I learn to ask: what incentives were they responding to?

4. A while ago I became a connoisseur of Chinese webnovels. Among those written for a male audience, there is a surprisingly diverse set

of character traits represented among the main characters. Doubtless many are womanizing murderhobos with no redeeming qualities, but others are classical heroes with big hearts, or sarcastic antiheroes who actually grow up a little, or ambitious empire-builders with grand plans to pave the universe with Confucian order, or down-on-their-luck starving artists who just want to bring happiness to the world through song.

If there is a single common virtue shared by all these protagonists, it is their *superhuman pain tolerance*. Protagonists routinely and often voluntarily dunk themselves in vats of lava, have all their bones broken, shattered, and reforged, get trapped inside alternate dimensions of freezing cold for millennia (which conveniently only takes a day in the outside world), and overdose on level-up pills right up to the brink of death, all in the name of becoming stronger. Oftentimes the defining difference between the protagonist and the antagonist is that the antagonist did not have enough pain tolerance and allowed the (unbearable physical) suffering in his life to drive him mad.

5. I have a close friend who often asks for my perspective on personal problems. A pattern arose in a couple of our conversations:

alkjash: I feel like you're not actually trying. [Meaning: using all the tools at your disposal, getting creative, throwing money at the problem to make it go away.]

alkjash's friend: What do you mean I'm not trying? I think I'm trying my best, can't you tell how hard I'm trying? [Meaning: piling on time, energy, and willpower to the point of burnout.]

After several of these conversations went nowhere, I learned that asking this friend to try harder directly translated in his mind to accusing him of low pain tolerance and asking him to hurt himself more.

II. Antidotes

I often hear on the internet laments like "Why is nobody actually trying?" Once upon a time, I was honestly and genuinely confused by this question. It seemed to me that "actually trying" - aiming the full force of your being at the solution of a problem you care about - is self-evidently motivating and requires zero extra justification if you care about the problem.

I think I finally understand why so few people are "actually trying." The reason is this pervasive and damaging belief that *pain is the unit of effort*. With this belief, the injunction "actually try" means "put yourself in as much pain as you can handle." Similarly, "she's trying her best" translates to "she's really hurting right now." Even worse, people with this belief *optimize for the appearance of suffering*. Answering emails at midnight and appearing fatigued at meetings are somehow taken to be more credible signals of effort than actual results. And if you think that's pathological, wait until you meet someone for whom *telling them about opportunities actively hurts them*, because you've just created another knife they feel pressured to cut themselves with.

I see a mob of people walking up to houses and throwing themselves bodily at the closed front doors. I walk up to block one man and ask, "Stop it! Why don't you try the doorknob first? Have you rung the doorbell?" The man responds in tears, nursing his bloody right shoulder, "I'm trying as hard as I can!" With his one good arm, he shoves me aside and takes a running start to lunge at the door again. Finally, the timber shatters and the man breaks through. The surrounding mob cheers him on, "Look how hard he's trying!"

Once you understand that pain is how people define effort, the answer to the question "why is nobody actually trying?" becomes astoundingly obvious. I'd like to propose two beliefs to counterbalance this awful state of affairs.

1. If it hurts, you're probably doing it wrong.

If your wrists ache on the bench press, you're probably using bad form and/or too much weight. If your feet ache from running, you might need sneakers with better arch support. If you're consistently sore for days after exercising, you should learn to stretch properly and check your nutrition.

Such rules are well-established in the setting of physical exercise, but their analogs in intellectual work seem to be completely lost on people. If reading a math paper is actively unpleasant, you should find a better-written paper or learn some background material first (most likely both). If you study or work late into the night and it disrupts your Circadian rhythm, you're trading off long-term productivity and well-being for low-quality work. That's just bad form.

If it hurts, you're probably doing it wrong.

2. You're not trying your best if you're not happy.

Happiness is really, really instrumentally useful. Being happy gives you more energy, increases your physical health and lifespan, makes you more creative and risk-tolerant, and (even if all the previous effects are unreplicated pseudoscience) causes other people to like you more. Whether you are tackling the Riemann hypothesis, climate change, or your personal weight loss, one of the first steps should be to acquire as much happiness as you can get your hands on. And the good news is: at least anecdotally[1], it is possible to substantially raise your happiness set-point through jedi mind tricks.

Becoming happy is a fully general problem-solving strategy. And although one can in principle trade off happiness for short bursts of productivity, in practice this is never worth it.

Culturally, we've been led to believe that over-stressed and tired people are the ones trying their best. It is right and proper to be kind to such people, but let's not go so far as to support the delusion that they are inputting as much effort as their joyful, boisterous peers bouncing off the walls.

You're not trying your best if you're not happy.

[Edit: Antidotes #1 and #2 are not primarily to be interpreted as truth claims, see Anna Salamon's comment on the original post[2].]

Endnotes

(1) Alicorn. Ureshiku Naritai. 8th Apr 2010.

(2) https://www.lesswrong.com/posts/bx3gkHJehRCYZAF3r/ pain-is-not-the-unit-of-effort?commentId=kZXYGXGdBjYGH- 6miC

Is success the enemy of freedom?

I. Parables

A. Anna is a graduate student studying p-adic quasicoherent topology. It's a niche subfield of mathematics where Anna feels comfortable working on neat little problems with the small handful of researchers interested in this topic. Last year, Anna stumbled upon a connection between her pet problem and algebraic matroid theory, solving a big open conjecture in the matroid Langlands program. Initially, she was over the moon about the awards and the Quanta articles, but now that things have returned to normal, her advisor is pressuring her to continue working with the matroid theorists with their massive NSF grants and real-world applications. Anna hasn't had time to think about p-adic quasicoherent topology in months.

B. Ben is one of the top Tetris players in the world, infamous for his signature move: the reverse double T-spin. Ben spent years perfecting this move, which requires lightning fast reflexes and nerves of steel, and has won dozens of tournaments on its back. Recently, Ben felt like his other Tetris skills needed work and tried to play online without using his signature move, but was greeted by a long string of losses: the Tetris servers kept matching him with the other top players in the world, who absolutely stomped him. Discouraged, Ben gave up on the endeavor and went back to practicing the reverse double T-spin.

C. Clara was just promoted to become the youngest Engineering Director at a mid-sized software startup. She quickly climbed the ranks, thanks to her amazing knowledge of all things object-oriented and her excellent communication skills. These days, she finds her schedule packed with what the company needs: back-to-back high-level strategy meetings preparing for the optics of the next product launch, instead of what she loves: rewriting whole codebases in Haskell++.

D. Deborah started her writing career as a small-time crime novelist, who split her time between a colorful cast of sleuthy protagonists. One day, her spunky children's character Detective Dolly blew up in popularity due to a Fruit Loops advertising campaign. At the beginning of every month, Deborah tells herself she's going to finally kill off Dolly and get to work on that grand historical romance she's been dreaming about. At the end of every month, Deborah's husband comes home with the mortgage bills for their expensive bayside mansion, paid for with "Dolly money," and Deborah starts yet another Elementary School Enigma.

E. While checking his email in the wee hours of the morning, Professor Evan Evanson notices an appealing seminar announcement: "A Gentle Introduction to P-adic Quasicoherent Topology (Part the

First)." Ever since being exposed to the topic in his undergraduate matroid theory class, Evan has always wanted to learn more. He arrives bright and early on the day of the seminar and finds a prime seat, but as others file into the lecture hall, he's greeted by a mortifying realization: it's a graduate student learning seminar, and he's the only faculty member present. Squeezing in his embarrassment, Evan sits through the talk and learns quite a bit of fascinating new mathematics. For some reason, even though he enjoyed the experience, Evan never comes back for Part the Second.

F. Whenever Frank looks back to his college years, he remembers most fondly the day he was kicked out of the conservative school newspaper for penning a provocative piece about jailing all billionaires. Although he was a mediocre student with a medium-sized drinking problem, on that day Frank felt like a *man with principles*. A real American patriot in the ranks of Patrick Henry or Thomas Jefferson. After college, Frank met a girl who helped him sort himself out and get sober, and now he's the proud owner of a small accounting firm and has two beautiful daughters Jenny and Taylor. Yesterday, arsonists set fire to the Planned Parenthood clinic across the street, and his employees have been clamoring for Frank to make a political statement. Frank almost threw caution to the wind and Tweeted #bodilyautonomy from the company account right there, but then the picture on his desk catches his eye: his wife and daughters at Taylor's elementary school graduation. It's hard to be a man of principles when you have something to lose.

G. Garrett is a popular radio psychologist who has been pressured by his sponsors into being the face of the yearly Breast Cancer Bike-a-thon. Unfortunately, Garrett has a dark secret: he's never ridden a bicycle. Too embarrassed to ask anyone for help or even be seen practicing—he is a respected public figure, for god's sake—Garrett buys a bike and sneaks to an abandoned lot to practice by himself after sunset. He thinks to himself, "how hard can it be?" Garrett shatters his ankle ten minutes into his covert practice session and has to pull out of the event. Fortunately, Garrett's sponsors find an actual celebrity to fill in for him and breast cancer donations reach record highs.

II. Motivation

What is personal success for?

We say success opens doors. Broadens horizons. Pushes the envelope. Shatters glass ceilings.

Success sets you free.

But what if it doesn't?

Take a good hard look at the successful people around you. Doctors too busy to see their children on weekdays. Mathematicians too brilliant in one field to switch to another. Businessmen too wealthy to avoid nightly wining and dining. Professional gamers too specialized to learn a new hero. Public figures too popular to change their minds.

Remember that time Michael Jordan took a break from basketball and played professional baseball[1]? They said he would have made an excellent professional player given time. Jordan said baseball was his childhood dream. Even so, in just over a year Jordan was back in basketball. It is hard not to imagine what a baseball player Michael Jordan could have been, *had he been less successful going in*.

I think it was in college that I first noticed *something wasn't right* about this picture. I spent my first semester studying and playing Go for about eight hours a day. I remember setting out a goban on the carpet of my dorm room and studying patterns in the morning as my roommate left for classes; when he returned to the room in the evening, he was surprised to see me still sitting there contemplating the flow of the stones. Because this was not the first or tenth time this had happened, he commented something like, "You must be really smart to not need to study."

I remember being dumbstruck by that statement. It suggested that my freedom to play board games for eight hours a day was gated by my personal success, and other Harvard students would be able to live like me *if only they were smarter.* But you know who else can play board games for eight hours a day? Basement-dwelling high school dropouts, who are—for all their unsung virtues—*definitely not smarter than Harvard students.*

When I entered college, they told me a Harvard education would empower me to do anything I want. The world would be my oyster. I took that message to heart in those four years—I fell in love, played every PC game that money could buy, studied programming languages and systems programming, and read more than one Russian novel. When I talked to my peers, however, I was constantly surprised at the overwhelming sameness of their ambitions. Four years later, twenty out of thirty-odd graduating seniors at our House planned to work in finance or consulting.

(Now, it could be that college really empowers these bright young scholars to realize their childhood dreams of arbitraging the yen against the kroner. But this is, as they say in the natural sciences, *definitely not the null hypothesis.*)

All of this would have made a teenager hate the idea of success altogether. I was not a teenager anymore, so I formulated a slightly more sophisticated answer: *Regardless of how successful I become, I resolve to live like a failure*.

This is a post about all the forces, real and imagined, that can make success the enemy of personal freedom. As long as these forces exist, and as long as the human heart yearns for liberty, few people will ever want wholeheartedly to succeed. Were it not already reality, that is a state of affairs too depressing to contemplate.

(Just to be clear, people are plenty motivated to succeed when basic needs are at stake—to put food on the table, to get laid, to pay for the mortgage. But after those needs get met, success just doesn't look all that great and only certain sorts of delightful weirdos keep striving. The rest of us mostly just lay back and enjoy the fruits of their labor.)

III. Factorization

I think all of the experiences in Section I can be summed up by the umbrella-term "Sunk Cost Fallacy," but that theory is a little too low-resolution$_2$ for my tastes. In this section I identify three main psychological factors of the phenomenon.

1. You rose to meet the challenge. Your peer group rose to meet you.

We are constantly sorted together with people of the same age group, at similar levels of competence, at similar stages in our careers. To keep up with the group, you have to run as fast as you can just to stay in place, as the saying goes. And if you run twice as fast as that, you just end up in a new, even harder-to-impress peer group. When your friends are all level 80, it's dreadfully difficult to restart at level 1.

Your friends may even be sympathetic, but it rarely helps matters.

Maybe you want to try something totally new, and your friends are too invested in their pet genre to emigrate with you.

Maybe you're excited to learn a new skill one of your hyper-competent friends is specialized in, and you ask them to coach you. Unfortunately, this turns out to be a massive mistake, because your friend only remembers how she got from level 75 to 80, and sort of assumes everything below is trivial. It's technically possible to learn area formulas as a special case of integral calculus, but only technically.

Maybe you transition to a new role within the team, you struggle to learn a new set of tricks, and you start hating yourself for not pulling as much weight as you're used to. You start to see a mix of pity and frustration in your teammates' eyes as you drag the whole team down.

2. Yesterday, you were bad at everything, and that really sucked. Today you're good at one thing, and you're hanging on for dear life.

It's hard to move out of your comfort zone when your comfort zone is one hundred square feet on top of Mount Olympus and every cardinal direction points straight off a cliff. Seems like just yesterday you stood at the base of this mountain among the rest of the mortals, craning your neck to get a peek at what it's like up here.

Kindly god-uncle Zeus calls a special thunderstorm for your arrival. Dionysus pours you a frothy drink and shares a bawdy tale. Hephaestus personally fashions you a blade as a symbol of your newfound status. Aphrodite invites you to her parlor for a night of good old-fashioned philosophy. They all act so welcoming, so natural, so in their element, and *you know you're only up here by a stroke of pure luck*.

When Hermes returns the next morning and invites you to fly with him on his winged boots to see the world, you decline graciously. Not because you don't want to—they're winged boots!—but because the moment you try anything out of the ordinary *you'll be found out for the impostor that you are* and god-uncle Zeus will show you his not-so-kindly side and chain you to a liver-eating eagle or a boulder that only obeys the laws of gravity intermittently.

3. Success gave you something to lose.

They say beware the man with nothing to lose.

I say envy him, because he alone is free.

You fondly recall the good old days of two thousand and two when you could go online and post diatribes against religion as a "militant atheist." In those days, you had nothing, and you were free. You were unattached. You were intellectually wealthy but financially insolvent. You could see one end of the place you call home from the other.

Now that you've made it big, you'd have to carefully position mirrors at the ends of three hallways to see that far. You're attached to wonderful person(s) of amenable sexual orientation(s). You have a reputation to maintain in the ever-smaller circles that you walk. Children in your community look up to you, or so you tell yourself. And so, even though deep in your heart you still believe that *only idiots believe in an old man in the sky,* your Twitter profile identifies you as "spiritual, yearning, exploring."

IV. Resolution?

It seems to me we have a problem.

We are not a species known for risk-taking[3], so human flourishing really depends on the explicit emphasis of exploration and openness to new experience. And yet it seems that the game is set up so that the most successful people are the least incentivized to explore further. That all the trying new things and pushing boundaries and calling for revolution is likely to come from those with neither the power to get it done nor the competence to do it correctly.

But it's not a hopeless case by any means. Many of the most successful people got there precisely by valuing freedom, creativity, and exploration, and still practice these values—so far as they can—within the confines of their walled gardens. We live in an information age where getting good at things is as easy as it's ever been. And at the very least we pay lip service to healthy adages like "Stay hungry, stay foolish."

But what does one do personally to maintain one's freedom?

I don't claim to have a fully general solution to this problem, but here is a rule that's helped me in the past.

When learning something new, treat yourself like a five-year-old.

If you've never spoken a word of Korean in your life, it doesn't matter if you're a professor of English Literature. As far as learning Korean goes, you're a five-year-old. Treat yourself like one. Make yourself a snack for memorizing the vertical vowels. Take a break after reading your first sentence and come back tomorrow. When you're done for the day, suck your thumb while staring at the first Korean word you've ever learned and feel the honest pride well up in your heart.

If you've never washed a dish in your life, it doesn't matter if you're a professional chef. As far as washing dishes is concerned, you're a five-year-old. Treat yourself like one. Make yourself a snack for figuring out how to dispense dish soap without getting it everywhere. Take a break after finishing the bowls and come back tomorrow. When you're all done, take a moment to take in that beautiful empty sink and feel the honest pride well up in your toddler heart.

Do you see how profoundly counterproductive it would be for the Korean learner to beat herself up for not being able to converse fluently with her Asian friends after two weeks? Do you see how completely unkind it would be for the novice dishwasher to call himself a useless piece of shit for not being able to execute the most basic of adult tasks?

Be kind to yourself and adjust your expectations to reality. When learning something new, treat yourself like a five-year-old.

Endnotes

(1) Steve Wulf. From the archives: The true story behind Michael Jordan's brief-but-promising baseball career. May 10th 2020.

(2) radimentary. High Resolution. 15th Dec 2017.

(3) Wikipedia. Risk aversion (psychology).

Zvi Mowshowitz

Simulacra levels and their interactions

Previously: Covid-19: My Current Model[1], On Negative Feedback and Simulacra[2]

This essay aims to unpack and explain simulacra levels of action using the threat of Covid-19 as its central example. My intention is for future posts to then apply this model to many Covid-related dynamics.

In Elizabeth's Negative Feedback and Simulacra[3], she examined several example situations in which information was being processed on multiple simulacra levels at once. On Negative Feedback and Simulacra was my take on those examples.

To re-familiarize ourselves with the simulacra levels, here's the introduction Elizabeth offered to them in her post:

> My friend Ben Hoffman[4] talks about simulacra a lot, with this rough definition:
>
> First, words were used to maintain shared accounting. We described reality intersubjectively in order to build shared maps, the better to navigate our environment. I say that the food source is over there, so that our band can move towards or away from it when situationally appropriate, or so people can make other inferences based on this knowledge.
>
> 2. The breakdown of naive intersubjectivity— people start taking the shared map as an object to be manipulated, rather than part of their own subjectivity. For instance, I might say there's a lion over somewhere where I know there's food, in order to hoard access to that resource for idiosyncratic advantage. Thus, the map drifts from reality, and we start dissociating from the maps we make.
>
> 3. When maps drift far enough from reality, in some cases people aren't even parsing it as though it had a literal specific objective meaning that grounds out in some verifiable external test outside of social reality. Instead, the map becomes a sort of command language[5] for coordinating actions and feelings. "There's food over there" is perhaps construed as a bid to move in that direction, and evaluated as though it were that call to action. Any argument for or against the implied call to action is conflated with

an argument for or against the proposition literally asserted. This is how arguments become soldiers[6]. Any attempt to simply investigate the literal truth of the proposition is considered at best naive and at worst politically irresponsible.

But since this usage is parasitic on the old map structure that was meant to describe something outside the system of describers, language is still structured in terms of reification and objectivity, so it substantively resembles something with descriptive power, or "aboutness." For instance, while you cannot acquire a physician's privileges and social role simply by providing clear evidence of your ability to heal others, those privileges are still justified in terms of pseudo-consequentialist arguments about expertise in healing.

4. Finally, the pseudostructure itself becomes perceptible as an object that can be manipulated, the pseudocorrespondence breaks down, and all assertions are nothing but moves in an ever-shifting game where you're trying to think a bit ahead of the others (for positional advantage), but not too far ahead.

If that doesn't make sense, try this anonymous comment[7] on the post

> Level 1: "There's a lion across the river." = There's a lion across the river.
>
> Level 2: "There's a lion across the river." = I don't want to go (or have other people go) across the river.

Level 3: "There's a lion across the river." = I'm with the popular kids who are too cool to go across the river.

Level 4: "There's a lion across the river." = A firm stance against trans-river expansionism focus grouped well with undecided voters in my constituency.

Almost everyone would rather not be eaten by a lion. I certainly would rather not be eaten by a lion.

Whether or not I am eaten by a lion still does not drive much of my decision making. It is highly implausible that I will be eaten by a lion.

I hope that if, in the future, it becomes plausible that I may get eaten by a lion, how to not get eaten by a lion would then drive much of my decision making.

If the presence of lions in various places would not put anyone in any danger, that makes it much less expensive for me to be wrong about where they are. The less people are concerned about the consequences of having or inflicting incorrect object-level models of the world, the less concerned they will be with Level 1 and with the Level 1 accuracy of their statements.

The prioritization of various simulacra levels becomes a habit. If you are used to interpreting "There's a lion across the river" almost entirely as "I'm with the popular kids who are too cool to go across the river" - because that's what it almost always means in your village - it may be very difficult for someone to say "No, really, I'm not associating with the cool kids right now. There's literally an actual lion across the actual river, and if you cross the river you will die."

There is no good way to sacrifice the cool points in order to communicate the presence of a lion. Even if it works at first, soon there will be a tendency for the new wording to become the canonical form of "I'm with the popular kids who are too cool to go across the river."

If everyone's instinct is to interpret "There's a lion across the river" as *both* "There is an actual lion across the actual river" and *also* "I'm with the kids who are too cool to cross the river" then there is a chance.

There is still a barrier. Whoever wants to share knowledge of the lion will become less cool by doing so. Ideally, for high enough stakes, this stops being a problem in multiple ways. If lives are at stake, especially one's own or one's loved ones, being cool looks less important than avoiding the lion. Ideally, being the person who saved us from the lion is also considered kind of cool, allowing one to both starve lions and look cool. That only works if everyone realizes the lion was there. But the payoff could be very large. So there's a chance.

Whereas, if things are too forsaken, one *loses the ability to communicate about the lion at all*. There is no combination of sounds one can make that makes people think there is an actual lion across an actual river that will actually eat them if they cross the river.

I'm not trying to be subtle here. You can guess where this is going.

There's a Virus Across The Ocean

Level 1

"There's a pandemic headed our way from China" means "there's a pandemic headed our way from China."

"There's no pandemic headed our way from China" means "there's **no** pandemic headed our way from China."

Level 2

"There's a pandemic headed our way from China" means "I want you to act as if you think there might be a pandemic on our way from China", while hoping to still be interpreted by the listener as meaning "There's a pandemic headed our way from China".

The speaker hopes to be interpreted as still meaning "There's a pandemic headed our way from China".

This may involve any of the following:

"I want you to click on this headline about a pandemic headed our way from China and/or subscribe to and share my newsletter, website or channel."

"I want you to have more negative affect towards China and/or other foreigners."

"I want you to be afraid."

"I want to shut down economic activity."

"I want to sell you toilet paper, masks and hand sanitizer at premium prices."

"I want you to thank me later for any or all of the above."

"There is no pandemic headed our way from China" means "I want you to act as if you think there is **not** a pandemic headed our way from China".

The speaker hopes to be interpreted as still meaning "There is not a pandemic headed our way from China".

This may include any of the following:

"I want you to click on this headline about there not being a pandemic headed our way from China and/or subscribe to and share my newsletter, website or channel."

"I want you to have more positive affect towards China and/or other foreigners."

"I do not want you to be afraid."

"I want to stop you from hoarding toilet paper, masks and hand sanitizer."

"I want to avoid shutting down economic activity."

"I want you to thank me later for any or all of the above."

Level 1 vs. Level 2

The key differences are in the intended effect of the statement made and to what extent the statement is correlated with the true state of the physical world.

Level 2 statements *do not have to be untrue, n*or need it be something you do not believe. It is often said that "the truth is the best lie."

Nor need the statement be selfish, as many Level 2 statements really are intended *for the subject's "own good"*.

What makes a statement Level 2 rather than Level 1 is that *you don't care whether or not it is true*. Instead, you care about what actions it causes people to take and whether or not you like those actions.

If there is a *tiger* across the river, but the group is insufficiently afraid of tigers, you might claim there is a lion across the river instead.

If there is a tiger across the river, but you have a shotgun and are itching to get a tiger's head as a trophy, you might claim there is not a lion across the river, so that we will cross the river. Whether or not you are aware of a lion across the river doesn't matter. A lion would prevent you from hunting tigers. You want to hunt a tiger.

The Four Direct Communicators

Sticking to the first two levels for now, we can divide into quadrants and see five types of communication strategies.

Let V = "There is a virus across the ocean that is likely to cause a pandemic here."

Let ~V = "There is not a virus across the ocean that is likely to cause a pandemic here."

Let C = The consequences of being told V.

Let ~C = The consequences of being told ~V.

Let N = The consequences of being told nothing. For simplicity assume everyone either believes that C>N, or that ~C>N.

The Oracle only looks at Level 1. The Oracle says V if and only if the Oracle believes V with sufficient confidence, says ~V if they believe ~V with sufficient confidence, and says nothing or "I don't know" otherwise. They care not whether C>~C or ~C>C.

The Trickster only looks at Level 2. The Trickster says V if they think C>~C. They say ~V if they think ~C>C. Otherwise they say nothing. They care not whether V is true.

The Nihilist cares about neither Level 1 nor Level 2. They say whatever they feel like saying, then eat at Arby's[8].

The Sage looks at *both* Level 1 and Level 2 and avoids actions that violate either principle. They say V if *both* they believe V *and* they believe C>~C. They say ~V if *both* they believe ~V *and* they believe ~C>C. If they believe that V but ~C>C, or they believe that ~V but C>~C, they say nothing.

The Pragmatist looks at *both* Level 1 and Level 2 and assigns some value to each, then takes action that balances both concerns. They recognize that there is a cost to saying that which is not, but that cost is not infinite. Thus, if the Sage would talk, they talk. If the Sage would not talk, they may talk anyway. Up to a point, they'll speak the truth and take the direct consequences even if those consequences are bad. Past a certain point, they'll be willing to lie.

There's obviously a continuum all around, especially between Sage and Pragmatists. *Almost* everyone has *some* breaking point where they would lie for a sufficiently powerful cause. *Most* people place value on telling the truth beyond known specific and direct consequences, and thus it takes some threshold of bad other consequences to get them to be quiet.

Once you know which of these types a person is, you can trust them in some sense.

It's easy to interpret an Oracle or a Sage. When a Sage is silent, you can trust that either they don't know the answer, or they believe telling you the answer would be bad. Often, absent strong glomarization[9], this lets you figure out the answer.

But it's also easy, *once you know they're a Trickster*, to trust a Trickster in their own way. You simply interpret their statements as manipulations rather than observations.

Level 3

"There's a pandemic headed our way from China" means "I wish to associate with the group that claims there is a pandemic headed our way from China."

This may include any of the following:

"I want to affirm my membership in my in-group and that I dislike the out-group."

"I want to be part of the group of people with power and/or who are winning."

"I want to be seen serving those with power and spreading their messages."

"I want to be seen as smart, on the ball, ahead of the curve, scientific and other neat stuff like that."

"I want to be part of the group that cares about people."

"I want to be part of the group that believes/defies experts."

"I want to be part of the group of so-called 'responsible experts' on this."

"I want to be part of the group that isn't afraid to tell you hard truths."

"I want to be part of the group that doesn't have bad traits like racism."

"The high status move is to endorse this position at this time."

"The publication I write for wants to hear this."

And so on.

"There's no pandemic headed our way from China" means "I wish to associate with the group that claims there is **not** a pandemic headed our way from China."

It may include any or all of exactly the same things, depending on your local situation and where you are in the timeline.

The polarity of many of these motivations has changed. In some cases, it has changed multiple times.

Level 4

"There's a pandemic headed our way from China" means "It is advantageous for me to say there is a pandemic headed our way from China."

"This set of verbal incantations focuses attention *on* places where focused attention helps me and *away* from places where focused attention hurts me."

"This set of verbal incantations will make people think I am associated and allied with those for whom it is advantageous to think I am associated and allied with."

"This set of verbal incantations associates me with good words and emotions, or my enemies with bad words and emotions."

"It would be advantageous for me if the group I am associated with is viewed as advocating the claim that there is a pandemic headed our way from China."

"This claim fits the heuristics of claims that will make me look responsible."

"This claim fits the heuristics of claims that will make me look strong and/or powerful and/or in the know and/or a winner."

"This claim fits the heuristics of claims that give one leverage and/or power."

"This claim fits the heuristics of claims that will make me someone others think that others will view as a valuable ally, especially others also operating at Level 4."

"This claim fits the heuristics of claims that will stop me from being scapegoated."

"This claim fits the heuristics of creating optionality and/or of putting rivals and opponents into situations where they will look bad."

"There's no pandemic headed our way from China" means the same thing, except in this situation the additional incantation "no" seems appropriate.

Note that the Level 4 actor has, in an important sense, lost the ability to think or plan.

It might or might not impact this calculation whether or not your statement is true (Level 1), or whether it will be believed (Level 2), or what coalitions this statement signals your membership in or support of (Level 3). The primary way in which Level 1+2 considerations impact this decision is indirectly, through their impact on Level 3.

That's all part of a calculation and matters only to the extent that it affects the consequences of saying the thing.

I find Level 4 is the hardest to grok, by far. It does not come naturally to me.

A potentially easier way to understand Level 4 is to think about how it fits into the contrasts between the first three levels, as will now be discussed.

Level 1 vs. Level 2 vs. Level 3

Consider the first three levels of action and consequence. Level 1 cares about the object level. Level 2 cares about the consequences of changing perception of the object level. Level 3 cares about which coalition your statement associates you with, and which coalitions would approve or disapprove of your statement.

We can think of each of the possible three contrasts. Is Oceania at war with East Asia, Eurasia or both?

We can then add Level 4 into the mix, wherever it belongs based on that division.

Level 1 vs. Levels 2+3+4: Truth versus Untruth

This division feels the most natural to me and people similar to me. Here, Level 4 actions definitely fall into the 2+3 camp, with this full division being Level 1 vs. Levels 2+3+4.

Level 1 statements correspond to object-level truth. If everyone makes Level 1 statements, everyone's map improves. Decisions get better. Action that has good object-level consequences can be taken. People can be trusted in a pure sense.

Higher level statements corrupt all that. Trust is destroyed. People's beliefs no longer converge towards the truth. Actions taken are what those with power - those who manipulate and form alliances more effectively - think they want to happen. Since they don't have the true picture of the situation either, they often don't like those consequences and regret their choices to the extent that they care about those consequences.

What difference, this perspective asks, does it make whether you said "Don't prepare, there's nothing to worry about" because you wanted to save masks for health care workers, or be able to buy up all the hand sanitizer for resale, or because you were worried about prejudice against Asians, or you wanted to keep the economy open, or you wanted to look responsible and calming rather than irresponsible and alarmist, or that's what all the authoritative media and government sources were saying and you wanted to be seen as someone who holds the party line(or, at Level 4, if you believe that it will increase the power of your group to be seen as advocating for this position, because it will improve your image or it is popular)?

From this perspective, the only important thing is, *you didn't care if what you said was true.* You said it, because it was useful to you to say it. That's what matters.

Thus, we can repeat the 2×2 from above. The only difference is now "the consequences" include coalition politics and other more abstract things.

It is easy to see why primarily Level 1 activities are helpful in dealing with Covid-19. It is also easy to see why one might view all primarily Level 2, 3 and 4 activities as assumed to be unhelpful.

Level 1+3 vs. Levels 2+4: Authentic vs. Inauthentic

This division can definitely be weird when first pointed out or considered, but it makes a decent amount of sense.

If I say that V, because I want to show that I am a member of the group that believes V, then that is a signal of group membership rather than evidence for V. But one can see this as an *authentic* signal of group membership. I *really do* wish to associate with the V-advocates and not with the anti-Vs.

The risk when sending this signal honestly is that one can confuse my statement of group membership with a claim of V.

I can be making an "honest" statement about which coalition I am supporting, and you can get the wrong impression that V is true.

Or, I could be making an honest statement that V, and you could get the impression that I wish to belong to the V-advocating coalition. This also distorts my map of reality in a potentially dangerous way.

If you can tell when someone is engaging in Level 3 actions versus Level 1 actions, then one can preserve the sanctity and trustworthiness of the Level 1 actions.

The Oracle who only cares about Level 1 is easy to interpret.

So is **The Drone**, who only cares about Level 3 and will be discussed below. The Drone's claim tells you their belief of what their side is currently advocating. No more, no less.

Alternatively, one can be an advocate for a side that presents the case in the best possible light, while only making true statements. This is a variation on the 1+2 strategy of the Sage. One can call this communication strategy **the Lawyer**. The Lawyer will say only things that have positive impact on Level 1 *and* positive impact on Level 3. Alternatively, they might say only things that have positive impact on

Level 1 *and* positive combined impact on Levels 2 and 3. Or they might need to fulfill all three requirements.

By contrast, statements on Level 2 or Level 4 can be entirely false.

Level 2 does this to manipulate your Level 1 map, and therefore your actions.

Level 4 does this as part of a system that manipulates your Level 3 map, and therefore your actions, believing that this is what drives human action.

If such considerations can dominate, or frequently do, then everything becomes a game.

In this perspective, primarily Level 3 actions are a positive driving force. Such considerations can motivate humans to align with accurate maps and helpful behaviors, under at least some conditions where pure object-level considerations would not work. This is one way we coordinate around washing our hands, locking down or wearing a mask.

Whereas Level 2 and Level 4 actions distort that, leading to inaccurate maps and unhelpful actions.

Levels 1+2 vs. Levels 3+4: Facts vs. Politics

This is natural, in the sense that it's higher levels versus lower levels. One can view the first two levels as *caring about the object level at all*.

You might lie. But you're lying because truth matters, beliefs determine physical actions and actions have consequences. Your desire for actions that follow from bad maps of the underlying territory is unfortunate. But at least there are maps of the territory involved, however flawed, and people are trying to cause actions that have consequences they themselves want to occur - even if those consequences are not good for others.

One can view Level 2 statements and actions as a sort of corruption of Level 1, but one still grounded in reality. They're fighting dirty, but they're still fighting. One can still speak one's mind; there is still a marketplace of ideas and, over time, truth retains a competitive advantage.

Whereas Level 3 is an entirely different thing, which has nothing but contempt for the idea that facts matter or that actions have consequences distinct from how they are viewed by others.

Hence the claim that "Facts Don't Matter."

Facts Don't Matter signifies that it does not matter if it is common knowledge that someone is lying.

Thus, Facts Don't Matter is the dominance of level 3+4 considerations over level 1+2 considerations. Why should I care if the words I say correspond accurately to the physical world's past, present or future? What matters is their impact on my membership in my coalition, and the success of myself and that coalition in playing political games.

An embodiment of this distinction is the resonance of the statement "I Demand A Plausible Lie$_{10}$". This is a request to cease purely Level 3+4 behavior and at least adapt some Level 2 considerations. It insists that one be allowed to maintain a map of reality, at all, outside of politics and that political considerations be bound at least a little by reality.

To the purely political actor, the implausible lie is better. If the lie is implausible, then those repeating it have sent a costly signal of loyalty and cut ties with lower levels. You don't have to worry that they repeated the statement because it happens to match the physical world or that they will refuse to repeat the next one if it fails to match.

Note also that if you only are playing politics, you might be able to act directly in a way that has a direct effect. What you cannot do is make or carry out physical plans involving multiple steps. In the best of times actually planning is very hard. This makes it impossible.

Levels 1+2+4 vs. Level 3: The Drone vs. The Agent

When grouping Levels 1+2 against Level 3, it feels natural to me to put Level 4 with Level 3. When talking about this with Ben Hoffman, it became clear there was also a view where it is Level 3 rather than Level 4 that feels alien and hard to grok, a view that naturally groups Level 4 with the first two levels instead.

In this view, the Drone, who cares only about Level 3 considerations, is the odd one out.

Anyone acting on any other level is an *agent*. They are *acting on* systems. Level 1 acts upon the physical world. Level 2 acts upon other people's models of the physical world. Level 4 acts upon people's models of other people and their dynamics.

Whereas the Drone lacks agency and free will entirely. The Drone does what they see others in their group are doing, says what others in their group are saying. More than anyone else, the Drone is a dead player.

Levels 1+2+3 vs. Level 4: The People vs. The Lizards

One could also group the first three levels together and contrast them with the fourth. This thinking is that there is ordinary decent interaction - humans being human - as represented by the first three levels. Then there are the schemers who prey upon us, twist everything in their sick games and play us against each other. We vote for the Lizards, as Douglas Adams reminds us, because if we don't, the wrong lizard might win.

The Lizards do not care about Covid-19. It would be a category error to say that the Lizards care about things at all. That implies they believe in the existence of things, or prefer one state of those things to another state, and act upon that in some way. That's not their jam.

Instead of having goals and trying to achieve them, the Lizards have systems of power accumulation. They follow habits of behavior that move away from potentially blameworthy actions towards ones that will be seen as good to sculpt perception of them as powerful and their opponents as weak, and so on. On multiple levels they have a complete inability to plan, even more so than in the last section. They are the Politician who prepares two speeches, one pro and one anti, and gives whichever sounds better.

This perspective says the problem is mainly the Lizards—or, alternatively, that you want to make sure you are one of the Lizards. Get rid of the Lizards, and you won't get a paradise, but you'll get systems that move towards truth and justice, that can plan and do useful things.

A Gentle Glossary of Strategies

From here, L-1 is Level 1, L-2 is Level 2, L-3 is Level 3, L-4 is Level 4.

Let's summarize the players. This is what they would say. What they would do is similar.

These players are roles that individuals take in situations. Few people will embody one of them at all times in all circumstances. Sometimes you see a lion across the river.

Nothing: The Nihilist says some things, then eats at Arby's.

L-1: The Oracle speaks the truth, even if their voice trembles.

L-2: The Trickster says that which causes beliefs that cause the actions they want.

L-1 and L-2: The Sage says only true things that don't have bad consequences.

L-3: The Drone sings songs and carries signs, mostly saying hurray for our side.

L-1 and L-3: The Lawyer says the true things that comprise the best argument for their position.

L-3 and L-4: The Politician ignores the object level and only considers politics.

L-4: The Lizard trusts their instincts and does that which creates or captures power.

L-All: The Pragmatist balances impact at all levels they are aware of slash care about when deciding what to say.

Several of these roles have important divisions into two or more related-but-distinct approaches. A key question is whether considerations act as veto points or if they are weighed against each other. Further discussion is beyond scope here, but I hope it happens in the future.

(I think this is missing 1-3 additional roles. Discussion question: What is the Idealist?)

Paths Forward

All actions and statements operate on all four levels at once, to the extent that they have implications on those levels.

The *intent* of a statement is often entirely on one level. That's not how humans or Bayesians interpret an action. If you want to improve the physical world without having any higher-level side effects, that's going to require extra effort. Avoiding meaningful implications on levels 2, 3 and 4 is *hard work*. The same bleeding effect occurs when aiming for higher levels as well. For concrete discussion of this, see my previous essayon simulacra levels.

As I say in the previous section, many of these roles have multiple variations and a lot of complexity inside them. Posts that explore them in detail would be worthwhile.

There is also the issue of the overall simulacra level of a group, organization or civilization. What is the default interpretation of information or action? What is the assumed motivation? What does that say about the group's dynamics and its ability to do things? I'm still trying to work through these things. There's clearly a somewhat distinct way of thinking about 3rd and 4th Level simulacra that is built around these questions, rather than thinking about individual actions. I *suspect* that the two are fully compatible and describe aspects of the same thing, but I'm still working that out and will talk about it more when I better understand it.

It's also possible there are two or more different models that are using the same four-level language structure, that share their concepts of Levels 1 and 2 but disagree about how Level 4 works, and to some extent, about Level 3. The more we talk about it, and the more concrete we can make our examples, the better we can sort all this out. The important thing is to get models that are useful.

The original intent of this post was to go on to analysis of other issues surrounding Covid-19. I was hoping to make clear what I meant by the more disputed statements in my Covid-19 model summary[11] from late March 2020, how and why I believe those dynamics occurred and what dynamics one can expect going forward. But this essay is long enough, so I've pushed that into the future.

Endnotes

(1) https://thezvi.wordpress.com/2020/05/31/covid-19-my-current-model/

(2) https://thezvi.wordpress.com/2020/05/03/on-negative-feed-back-and-simulacra/

(3) Elizabeth. Negative Feedback and Simulacra. 28th Apr 2020.

(4) http://benjaminrosshoffman.com/

(5) http://benjaminrosshoffman.com/actors-and-scribes-words-and-deeds/

(6)Eliezer Yudkowsky. Politics is the Mind-Killer. 18th Feb 2007.

(7) https://www.lesswrong.com/posts/fEX7G2N7CtmZQ3eB5/sim-ulacra-and-subjectivity?commentId=FgajiMrSpY9MxTS8b

(8) https://www.youtube.com/watch?v=6vxQqdFOeoM

(9) Wikipedia. Glomar response.

(10) https://dilbert.com/strip/1999-04-11

(11) https://thezvi.wordpress.com/2020/05/31/covid-19-my-current-model/

Zvi Mowshowitz

The Road to Mazedom

The previous essays in this sequence mostly took mazes as given.

As an individual, one's ability to fight any large system is limited.

That does not mean our individual decisions do not matter. They do matter. They add up.

Mostly our choice is a basic one. Lend our strength to that which we wish to be free from[1]. Or not do so.

Even that is difficult. The methods of doing so are unclear. Mazes are ubiquitous. Not lending our strength to mazes, together with the goal of keeping one's metaphorical soul intact and still putting food on the table, is already an ambitious set of goals for an individual in a world of mazes.

We now shift perspective from the individual to the system as a whole. We stop taking mazes as given.

It is time to ask *why* and *how* all of this happens, and what if anything we can do, individually or collectively, about it.

In particular, this essay presents an explicit model of the first question, which is:

How did mazes come to be, both individually and overall?

This is partly a summary of the model developed so far. It is partly making the model more explicit, and partly the fleshing out of that model with more gears.

1. Every organization has an organizational culture. That culture can and does change.

2. Those who focus on their own advancement at the expense of other considerations will, by default, advance further, faster and more often. Those who do not do this will not advance. Increasing amounts of focus make this effect increasingly large.

3. Focus on one's own advancement inside hierarchies causes individuals to self-modify in order to be the type of person who automatically engages in maze-creating and maze-supporting behaviors. They will also see such behavior as natural and virtuous.

4. Middle management performance is inherently difficult to assess. Maze behaviors systematically compound this problem. They strip away points of differentiation beyond loyalty to the maze and willingness to sacrifice one's self on its behalf, plus politics. Information and records are destroyed. Belief in the possibility of

differentiation in skill level, or of object-level value creation, is destroyed.

5. The more one is already within a maze, the more one is rewarded for maze-creating and maze-supporting behaviors, and for self-modifications towards such behaviors. This creates a vicious cycle.

6. Focus on one's own advancement causes one to wish to ally with others who do the same thing. That means allying with those who are engaging in maze-creating behaviors, and who are likely to do so in the future. Those people are likely to have future power. They are aligned in support of your new values and likely actions.

7. Changing the organizational culture towards a maze, which we will call *raising the maze level,* benefits those who wish to engage in maze-like behavior at the expense of those who do not. Those wishing to raise maze levels implicitly, and sometimes explicitly, coordinate together to reward maze behaviors, culture and values, and punish other behaviors, cultures and values.

8. Those who wish to have strong allies notice that strong potential allies want to ally with those who support mazes, and with those who ally with those who support mazes, and so on. This creates a strong incentive to strongly signal, in a way that others who support mazes can recognize, our support for maze behaviors and rising maze levels. One does this by supporting maze behaviors and maze allies whenever possible over all other considerations, without any need for explicit coordination or reciprocity, and by other costly signals of maze virtue.

9. The larger an organization and the more of a maze it becomes, the closer competition among its middle managers resembles super-perfect competition$_2$ plus political considerations. Slack$_3$ is destroyed. Those who refuse to get with the program, where the essence of the program

is support of mazes over non-mazes, stop getting promoted or are pushed out entirely.

10. Maze behaviors dictate how to react to people largely by observing those people's culture and values. Those who wish to get ahead in such worlds must self-modify to instinctively support such actions, whether or not doing so is locally in their self interest. Being too aware of one's local self-interest is therefore not in one's broader self-interest. Humans are much better at doing all this, and at detecting if others are doing it, than they are at faking it. The way one gets such behavior is through cultivating habits, including habits of thought, and choosing one's virtues. This self-modification creates even stronger implicit coordination.

11. There are contravening forces that can potentially outweigh all these effects, and result in maze behaviors being net punished. But they require those opposed to maze behaviors, culture and values to devote substantial resources to the cause, and to bear substantial costs. The more of a maze a place has already become, the harder it will be to turn things around or even stop things from getting worse. If such efforts are to succeed, this needs to be a high priority.

12. Even if maze behaviors are net punished for now, those who have embraced the maze nature will be skeptical of this. Even if they observe such behaviors being net punished now, they will not expect this to continue. Given the state of our world and culture, this is a highly reasonable prior. They also have knowledge of their own maze nature and presence within the organization, which is likely to raise maze levels over time and is evidence that the fight against mazedom is failing. And they stand to gain a huge competitive edge by raising the local maze level. Thus, the fight never ends.

13. Damage done is very difficult to reverse. Once particular maze behaviors become tolerated and levels rise, it takes a lot of effort to undo that.

14. Once people who support mazes are in places of authority in a given area, that area will rapidly become a maze. This is true of organizations, and of sub-organizations within an organization.

15. If the head of an organization believes in mazes, and has the time to choose and reward the people of their choice, it's all over. Probably permanently.

16. Mazes reward individuals who engage in maze behaviors and exhibit maze culture and values, and punish those who do not so exhibit, even outside the maze or organization in question. This includes customers, producers, business partners, investors and venture capitalists, board members, analysts, media, government officials, academics, and anyone else who supports or opposes such patterns.

17. All strengthening of mazes anywhere creates additional force supporting mazes elsewhere. Mazes instinctively support other mazes. As society falls increasingly under the sway of mazes, it implicitly cooperates to push everyone and everything into supporting the behaviors, culture, and values of mazes.

18. The end result inside any given organization is that maze behaviors grow stronger and more common over time. This is balanced by maze behaviors making the organization less effective, and thus more likely to fail.

19. Occasionally an organization can successfully lower its maze level and change its culture, but this is expensive and rare heroic behavior. Usually, this requires a bold leader and getting rid of a lot of people,

and the old organization is effectively replaced with a new one, even if the name does not change. A similar house cleaning happens more naturally in the other direction when and as maze levels rise.

20. Maze behaviors grow stronger and more common over time in any given organization barring rare heroic efforts. As organizations get bigger and last longer, maze levels increase.

21. When interacting with a world of low maze levels, or especially when interacting with individuals who have not embraced the maze nature, mazes are at a large competitive disadvantage versus non-mazes. Organizations with too-high maze levels become more likely to fail.

22. As organizations fail and are replaced by smaller upstarts via creative destruction, revolution, or other replacement, maze levels decrease.

23. Replacement of old organizations with new ones is the primary way maze levels decline.

24. As the overall maze level rises, mazes gain a competitive advantage over non-mazes.

25. If society sufficiently rewards mazes and punishes non-mazes, non-mazes can stop failing less often than mazes. Existing organizations become increasingly propped up by corruption. New organizations will start off increasingly maze-like, signal their intent to become mazes, and raise their maze levels more rapidly. They will still usually start out at much lower maze levels than old organizations.

26. New organizations and smaller organizations also have more benefit in survival and growth from non-maze behaviors versus maze

behaviors, as they have a greater need to do things mazes cannot do, or that they cannot do without huge additional overhead. Even in the scenario where large organizations benefit from maze coordination more than they are hurt by maze inefficiency, it can still benefit smaller organizations to minimize maze levels.

27. Mazes have reason to and do obscure that they are mazes, and to obscure the nature of mazes and maze behaviors. This allows them to avoid being attacked or shunned by those who retain enough conventional not-reversed values that they would recoil in horror from such behaviors if they understood them, and potentially fight back against mazes or attempt to lower maze levels. The maze-embracing individuals also take advantage of those who do not know of the maze nature. It is easy to see why the organizations described in *Moral Mazes* would prefer people not read the book *Moral Mazes*.

28. Simultaneously with pretending to the outside not to be mazes, those within them will claim if challenged that everybody knows they are mazes and how mazes work.

29. As maze levels rise, mazes take control of more and more of an economy and people's lives.

30. Under sufficiently strong pressure the maze behaviors, values, and culture filter out into the broader society. Maze behaviors, values, and culture are seen increasingly as legitimate, comfortable, and praiseworthy. This happens even outside of any organization. Non-maze behaviors are increasingly seen as illegitimate, uncomfortable, and blameworthy.

31. The result of these effects is that people in societies with high maze levels, especially those with power and wealth, increasingly and increasingly openly oppose and vilify the creation of clarity, engaging

in any productive object-level action, and participation in or even belief in the existence of positive-sum games of any kind. Simulacrum levels$_4$ continue to rise.

32. Given sufficiently high societal maze levels, talk in support of maze behaviors would eventually becoming more and more open, and dominate discourse and how people are educated about the world, as people explicitly and publicly endorse and teach anti-virtues over virtues.

33. We would see increasing societal inability to create clarity, engage in actions or do anything other than repeat existing patterns. Costs to all still possible actions would rise. Existing patterns would expropriate increasing portions of remaining resources to keep themselves afloat, and increasingly ban any activity outside those patterns.

34. The default outcome on the scale of individual organizations is the rise and fall of those organizations over time.

35. The default short term outcome on the scale of a nation, when maze levels and simulacrum levels increase, is declining growth, dynamism, slack, discourse, hope, happiness, virtue and wealth. People increasingly lose the things that matter in life.

36. The default long term outcome on the scale of a nation is the rise and fall of civilizations.

37. We do in fact see all of this. Here and now.

The next few essays in the sequence will flesh this out more and provide, as best I can, answers to the other questions.

Endnotes

(1) Jewel (song). Life Uncommon.

(2) Zvi Mowshowitz. Perfect Competition. 29th Dec 2019.

(3) Zvi Mowshowitz. Slack. 30th Sep 2017.

(4) Jean Baudrillard. Simulacra and Simulation. 1981.

Motive ambiguity

This is a central theme in: Immoral Mazes Sequence[1], but it generalizes.

W hen looking to succeed, pain is not the unit of effort[2], and money is a, if not the, unit of caring[3].

One is not always looking to succeed.

Here is a common type of problem.

You are married, and want to take your spouse out to a romantic dinner. You can choose the place your spouse loves best, or the place you love best.

A middle manager is working their way up the corporate ladder, and must choose how to get the factory to improve its production of widgets. A middle manager must choose how to improve widget production. He can choose a policy that improperly maintains the factory and likely eventually poisons the water supply, or a policy that would prevent that but at additional cost.

A politician can choose between a bill that helps the general population, or a bill that helps their biggest campaign contributor.

A start-up founder can choose between building a quality product without technical debt, or creating a hockey stick graph that will appeal to investors.

You can choose to make a gift yourself. This would be expensive in terms of your time and be lower quality, but be more thoughtful and cheaper. Or you could buy one in the store, which would be higher quality and take less time, but feel generic and cost more money.

You are cold. You can buy a cheap scarf, or a better but more expensive scarf.

These are trade-offs. Sometimes one choice will be made, sometimes the other.

Now consider another type of problem.

You are married, and want to take your spouse out to a romantic dinner. You could choose a place you both love, or a place that only they love. You choose the place you don't love, so they will know how much you love them. After all, you didn't come here for the food.

A middle manager must choose how to improve widget production. He can choose a policy that improperly maintains the factory and likely eventually poisons the water supply, or a policy that would prevent that at no additional cost. He knows that when he is up for promotion, management will want to know the higher ups can count on him to make the quarterly numbers look good and not concern himself with long-term issues or what consequences might fall on others. If he cared about not poisoning the water supply, he would not be a reliable political ally. Thus, he chooses the neglectful policy.

A politician can choose between two messages that affirm their loyalty: Advocating a beneficial policy, or advocating a useless and wasteful policy. They choose useless, because the motive behind advocating a beneficial policy is ambiguous. Maybe they wanted people to benefit!

A start-up founder can choose between building a quality product without technical debt and creating a hockey stick graph with it, or building a superficially similar low-quality product with technical debt and using that. Both are equally likely to create the necessary graph, and both take about the same amount of effort, time and money. They choose the low-quality product, so the venture capitalists can appreciate their devotion to creating a hockey stick graph.

You can choose between making a gift and buying a gift. You choose to make a gift, because you are rich and buying something from a store would be meaningless. Or you are poor, so you buy something from a store, because a handmade gift wouldn't show you care.

Old joke: One Russian oligarch says, "Look at my scarf! I bought it for ten thousand rubles." The other says, "That's nothing, I bought the same scarf for twenty thousand rubles."

What these examples have in common is that there is a strictly better action and a strictly worse action, in terms of physical consequences. In each case, the protagonist chooses the worse action *because it is worse*.

This choice is made as a costly signal. In particular, to avoid *motive ambiguity*.

If you choose something better over something worse, you will be suspected of doing so *because* it was better rather than worse.

If you choose something worse over something better, not only do you show how little you care about making the world better, you show that you care more *about people noticing and trusting this lack of caring*. It shows your values and loyalties.

In the first example, you care more about your spouse's view of how much you care about their experience than you care about your own experience.

In the second example, you care more about being seen as focused on your own success$_1$ than you care about outcomes you won't be responsible for.

In the third example, you care more about being seen as loyal$_4$ than about improving the world by being helpful.

In the fourth example, you care about those making decisions over your fate believing that you will focus on the things they believe the next person deciding your fate will care about$_5$, so they can turn a profit. They don't want you distracted by things like product quality.

In the old joke, the oligarchs want to show that they have money to burn, and that they care a lot about showing they have lots of money to burn. That they *actively want* to Get Got$_6$ to show they don't care. If someone thought the scarf was bought for mundane utility$_7$, that wouldn't do at all.

One highly effective way to get many people to spend money is to give them a choice to either spend the money, or be slightly socially awkward and admit that they care about not spending the money. Don't ask what the wine costs, it would ruin the evening.

The warning of Out to Get You[6] is insufficiently cynical. The motive is often not to get your resources, and is instead purely to make your life worse.

Conflict theorists[8] are often insufficiently cynical. We *hope* the war is about whether to enrich the wealthy or help the people. Often the war is over whether to aim to destroy the wealthy, or aim to hurt the people.

In simulacra terms[9], these effects are strongest when one desires to be seen as motivated on level three, but these dynamics are potentially present to an important extent for motivations at all levels. Note also that one is not motivated by this dynamic to destroy something unless you might plausibly favor it. If and only if everybody knows[10] you don't care about poisoning the river, it is safe to not poison it.

This generalizes to time, to pain, to every preference. Hence anything that wants your loyalty will do its best to ask you to sacrifice and destroy everything you hold dear, because you care about it, to demonstrate you care more about other things.

Worst of all, *none of this assumes a zero-sum mentality.* At all.

Such behavior *doesn't even need one*.

If one has a true zero-sum mentality, as many do, or one maps all results onto a zero-sum social dynamic, all of this is overthinking. All becomes simple. Your loss is my gain, so I want to cause you as much loss as possible.

Pain need not be the unit of effort if it is the unit of scoring.

The world would be better if people treated more situations like the first set of problems, and fewer situations like the second set of problems. How to do that?

Endnotes

(1) Zvi Mowshowitz. Mazes Sequence Summary. 23rd May 2020.

(2) alkjash. Pain is not the unit of Effort. 24th Nov 2020.

(3) Eliezer Yudkowsky. Money: The Unit of Caring. 31st Mar 2009.

(4) https://en.wikipedia.org/wiki/Pledge_of_Allegiance

(5) Zvi Mowshowitz. The Thing and the Symbolic Representation of The Thing. 30th June 2015.

(6) Zvi Mowshowitz. Out to Get You. 23rd Sept2017.

(7) https://tvtropes.org/pmwiki/pmwiki.php/Main/MundaneUtility

(8) Scott Alexander. Conflict vs. Mistake. 24th Jan 2018.

(9) Zvi Mowshowitz. Simulacra Levels and their Interactions.15th June 2020.

(10) Zvi Mowshowitz. Everybody Knows. 2nd Jul 2019.

Studies on Slack

I.

Imagine a distant planet full of eyeless animals. Evolving eyes is hard: they need to evolve Eye Part 1, then Eye Part 2, then Eye Part 3, in that order. Each of these requires a separate series of rare mutations.

Here on Earth, scientists believe each of these mutations must have had its own benefits[1]—in the land of the blind, the man with only Eye Part 1 is king. But on this hypothetical alien planet, there is no such luck. You need all three Eye Parts or they're useless. Worse, each Eye Part is metabolically costly; the animal needs to eat 1% more food per Eye Part it has. An animal with a full eye would be much more fit than anything else around, but an animal with only one or two Eye Parts will be at a small disadvantage.

So these animals will only evolve eyes in conditions of relatively weak evolutionary pressure. In a world of intense and perfect competition, where the fittest animal always survives to reproduce and the least fit always dies, the animal with Eye Part 1 will always die—it's less fit than its fully-eyeless peers. The weaker the competition, and the more randomness dominates over survival-of-the-fittest, the more likely an animal with Eye Part 1 can survive and reproduce long enough to eventually produce a descendant with Eye Part 2, and so on.

There are lots of ways to decrease evolutionary pressure. Maybe natural disasters often decimate the population, dozens of generations are spent recolonizing empty land, and during this period there's more than enough for everyone and nobody has to compete. Maybe there are frequent whalefalls[2], and any animal nearby has hit the evolutionary jackpot and will have thousands of descendants. Maybe the population is isolated in little islands and mountain valleys, and one gene or another can reach fixation in a population totally by chance. It doesn't matter exactly how it happens, it matters that evolutionary pressure is low.

The branch of evolutionary science that deals with this kind of situation is called "adaptive fitness landscapes". Landscapes really are a great metaphor—consider somewhere like this:

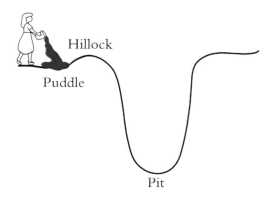

Hillock

Puddle

Pit

You pour out a bucket of water. Water "flows downhill", so it's tempting to say something like "water wants to be at the lowest point possible". But that's not quite right. The lowest point possible is the pit, and water won't go there. It will just sit in the little puddle forever, because it would have to go up the tiny little hillock in order to get to the pit, and water can't flow uphill. Using normal human logic, we feel tempted to say something like "Come on! The hillock is so tiny, and that pit is so deep, just make a single little exception to your 'always flow downhill' policy and you could do so much better for yourself!" But water stubbornly refuses to listen.

Under conditions of perfectly intense competition, evolution works the same way. We imagine a multidimensional evolutionary "landscape" where lower ground represents higher fitness. In this perfectly intense competition, organisms can go from higher to lower fitness, but never vice versa. As with water, the tiniest hillock will leave their potential forever unrealized.

Under more relaxed competition, evolution only *tends probabilistically* to flow downhill. Every so often, it will flow uphill; the smaller the hillock, the more likely evolution will surmount it. Given enough time, it's guaranteed to reach the deepest pit and mostly stay there.

Take a moment to be properly amazed by this. It sounds like something out of the Tao Te Ching. An animal with eyes has very high evolutionary fitness. It will win at all its evolutionary competitions. So in order to produce the highest-fitness animal, we need to—select for fitness less hard? In order to produce an animal that wins competitions, we need to stop optimizing for winning competitions?

This doesn't mean that less competition is always good. An evolutionary environment with no competition won't evolve eyes either; a few individuals might randomly drift into having eyes, but they won't catch on. In order to optimize the species as much as possible as fast as possible, you need the right balance, somewhere in the middle between total competition and total absence of competition.

In the esoteric teachings, total competition is called $Moloch_3$, and total absence of competition is called $Slack_4$. Slack (thanks to Zvi Mowshowitz for the term and concept) gets short shrift. If you think of it as "some people try to win competitions, other people don't care about winning competitions and slack off and go to the beach", you're misunderstanding it. Think of slack as a paradox—the Taoist art of winning competitions by not trying too hard at them. Moloch and Slack are opposites and complements, like yin and yang. Neither is stronger than the other, but their interplay creates the ten thousand things.

II.

Before we discuss slack further, a digression on group selection.

Some people would expect this discussion to be quick, since group selection doesn't exist. These people understand it as evolution acting for the good of a species. It's a tempting way to think, because evolution usually eventually makes species stronger and more fit, and sometimes we colloquially round that off to evolution targeting a species' greater good. But inevitably we find evolution is awful and does absolutely nothing of the sort.

Imagine an alien planet that gets hit with a solar flare once an eon, killing all unshielded animals. Sometimes unshielded animals spontaneously mutate to shielded, and vice versa. Shielded animals are completely immune to solar flares, but have 1% higher metabolic costs. What happens? If you predicted "magnetic shielding reaches fixation and all animals get it", you've fallen into the group selection trap. The unshielded animals outcompete the shielded ones during the long inter-flare period, driving their population down to zero (though a few new shielded ones arise every generation through spontaneous mutations). When the flare comes, only the few spontaneous mutants survive. They breed a new entirely-shielded population, until a few unshielded animals arise through spontaneous mutation. The unshielded outcompete the shielded ones again, and by the time of the next solar flare, the population is 100% unshielded again and they all die. If the animals are lucky, there will always be enough spontaneously-mutated shielded animals to create a post-flare breeding population; if they are unlucky, the flare will hit at a time with unusually few such mutants, and the species will go extinct.

An Evolution Czar concerned with the good of the species would just declare that all animals should be shielded and solve the problem. In the absence of such a Czar, these animals will just keep dying in solar-flare-induced mass extinctions forever, even though there is an easy solution with only 1% metabolic cost.

A less dramatic version of the same problem happens here on Earth. Every so often predators (let's say foxes) reproduce too quickly and outstrip the available supply of prey (let's say rabbits). There is a brief period of starvation as foxes can't find any more rabbits and die *en masse*. This usually ends with a boom-bust cycle[5]: after most foxes die, the rabbits (who reproduce very quickly and are now free of predation) have a population boom; now there are rabbits everywhere. Eventually the foxes catch up, eat all the new rabbits, and the cycle repeats again. It's a waste of resources for foxkind to spend so much of its time and energy breeding a huge population of foxes that will inevitably collapse a generation later; an Evolution Czar concerned with the common good would have foxes limit their breeding at a sustainable level. But since individual foxes that breed excessively are more likely to have their genes represented in the next generation than foxes that breed at a sustainable level, we end up with foxes that breed excessively, and the cycle continues.

(but humans are too smart to fall for this one, right?[6])

Some scientists tried to create group selection under laboratory conditions[7]. They divided some insects into subpopulations, then killed off any subpopulation whose numbers got too high, and "promoted" any subpopulation that kept its numbers low to better conditions. They hoped the insects would evolve to naturally limit their family size in order to keep their subpopulation alive. Instead, the insects became cannibals: they ate other insects' children so they could have more of their own without the total population going up. In retrospect, this makes perfect sense; an insect with the behavioral program "have many children, and also kill other insects' children" will have its genes better represented in the next generation than an insect with the program "have few children".

But sometimes evolution appears to solve group selection problems. What about multicellular life? Stick some cells together in a resource-plentiful environment, and they'll naturally do the evolutionary competition thing of eating resources as quickly as possible to churn out as many copies of themselves as possible. If you were expecting these cells to form a unitary organism where individual cells do things like become heart cells and just stay in place beating rhythmically, you would call the expected normal behavior "cancer" and be against it. Your opposition would be on firm group selectionist grounds: if any cell becomes cancer, it and its descendants will eventually overwhelm everything, and the organism (including all cells within it, including the cancer cells) will die. So for the good of the group, none of the cells should become cancerous.

The first step in evolution's solution is giving all cells the same genome; this mostly eliminates the need to compete to give their genes to the next generation. But this solution isn't perfect; cells can get mutations in the normal course of dividing and doing bodily functions. So it employs a host of other tricks: genetic programs telling cells to self-destruct if they get too cancer-adjacent, an immune system that hunts down and destroys cancer cells, or growing old and dying (this last one isn't usually thought of as a "trick", but it absolutely is: if you arrange for a cell line to lose a little information during each mitosis, so that it degrades to the point of gobbledygook after X divisions, this means cancer cells that divide constantly will die very quickly, but normal cells dividing on an approved schedules will last for decades).

Why can evolution "develop tricks" to prevent cancer, but not to prevent foxes from overbreeding, or aliens from losing their solar flare shields? Group selection works when the group itself has a shared genetic code (or other analogous ruleset) that can evolve. It doesn't work if you expect it to directly change the genetic code of each individual to cooperate more.

When we think of cancer, we are at risk of conflating two genetic codes: the shared genetic code of the multicellular organism, and the genetic code of each cell within the organism. Usually (when there are no mutations in cell divisions) these are the same. Once individual cells within the organism start mutating, they become different. Evolution will select for cancer in changes to individual cells' genomes over an organism's lifetime, but select against it in changes to the overarching genome over the lifetime of the species (ie you should expect all the genes you inherited from your parents to be selected against cancer, and all the mutations in individual cells you've gotten since then to be selected for cancer).

The fox population has no equivalent of the overarching genome; there is no set of rules that govern the behavior of every fox. So foxes can't undergo group selection to prevent overpopulation (there are some more complicated dynamics that might still be able to rescue the foxes in some situations, but they're not relevant to the simple model we're looking at).

In other words, group selection can happen in a two-layer hierarchy of nested evolutionary systems when the outer system (eg multicellular humans) includes rules that the inner system (eg human cells) have to follow, and where the fitness of the evolving-entities in the outer system depends on some characteristics of the evolving-entities in the inner system (eg humans are higher-fitness if their cells do not become cancerous). The evolution of the outer layer includes evolution over rulesets, and eventually evolves good strong rulesets that tell the inner-layer evolving entities how to behave, which can include group selection (eg humans evolve a genetic code that includes a rule "individual cells inside of me should not get cancer" and mechanisms for enforcing this rule).

You can find these kinds of two-layer evolutionary systems everywhere. For example, "cultural evolution" is a two-layer evolutionary system. In the hypothetical state of nature, there's unrestricted competition—people steal from and murder each other, and only the strongest survive. After they form groups, the groups compete with each other, and groups that develop rulesets that prevent theft and murder (eg legal codes, religions, mores) tend to win those competitions. Once again, the outer layer (competition between cultures) evolves groups that successfully constrains the inner layer (competition between individuals). Species don't have a czar who restrains internal competition in the interest of keeping the group strong, but some human cultures do (eg Russia).

Or what about market economics? The outer layer is companies, the inner layer is individuals. Maybe the individuals are workers—each worker would selfishly be best off if they spent the day watching YouTube videos and pushed the hard work onto someone else. Or maybe they're executives—each individual executive would selfishly be best off if they spent their energy on office politics, trying to flatter and network with whoever was most likely to promote them. But if all the employees loaf off and all the executives focus on office politics, the company won't make products, and competitors will eat their lunch. So someone—maybe the founder/CEO—comes up with a ruleset to incentivize good work, probably some kind of performance review system where people who do good work get promoted and people who do bad work get fired. The outer-layer competition between companies will select for corporations with the best rulesets; over time, companies' internal politics should get better at promoting the kind of cooperation necessary to succeed.

How do these systems replicate multicellular life's success without being literal entities with literal DNA having literal sex? They all involve a shared ruleset and a way of punishing rulebreakers which make it in each individual's short-term interest to follow the ruleset that leads to long-term success. Countries can do that (follow the law or we'll jail you), companies can do that (follow our policies or we'll fire you), even multicellular life can sort of do that (don't become cancer, or immune cells will kill you). When there's nothing like that (like the overly-fast-breeding foxes) evolution fails at group selection problems. When there is something like that, it has a chance. When there's something like that, and the thing like that is itself evolving (either because it's encoded in literal DNA, or because it's encoded in things like company policies that determine whether a company goes out of business or becomes a model for others), then it can reach a point where it solves group selection problems very effectively.

In the esoteric teachings, the inner layer of two-layer evolutionary systems is represented by the Goddess of Cancer, and outer layer by the Goddess of Everything Else$_8$. In each part of the poem, the Goddess of Cancer orders the evolving-entities to compete, but the Goddess of Everything Else recasts it as a two-layer competition where cooperation on the internal layer helps win the competition on the external layer. He who has ears to hear, let him listen.

III.

Why the digression? Because slack is a group selection problem. A species that gave itself slack in its evolutionary competition would do better than one that didn't—for example, the eyeless aliens would evolve eyes and get a big fitness boost. But no individual can unilaterally choose to compete less intensely; if it did, it would be outcompeted and die. So one-layer evolution will fail at this problem the same way it fails all group selection problems, but two-layer systems will have a chance to escape the trap.

The multicellular life example above is a special case where you want 100% coordination and 0% competition. I framed the other examples the same way—countries do best when their citizens avoid all competition and work together for the common good, companies do best when their executives avoid self-aggrandizing office politics and focus on product quality. But as we saw above, some systems do best somewhere in the middle, where there's some competition but also some slack.

For example, consider a researcher facing their own version of the eyeless aliens' dilemma. They can keep going with business as normal—publishing trendy but ultimately useless papers that nobody will remember in ten years. Or they can work on Research Program Part 1, which *might* lead to Research Program Part 2, which *might* lead to Research Program Part 3, which *might* lead to a ground-breaking insight. If their jobs are up for review every year, and a year from now the business-as-normal researcher will have five trendy papers, and the groundbreaking-insight researcher will be halfway through Research Program Part 1, then the business-as-normal researcher will outcompete the groundbreaking-insight researcher; as the saying goes, "publish or perish". Without slack, no researcher can unilaterally escape the system; their best option will always be to continue business as usual.

But group selection makes the situation less hopeless. Universities have long time-horizons and good incentives; they want to get famous for producing excellent research. Universities have rulesets that bind their individual researchers, for example "after a while good researchers get tenure". And since universities compete with each other, each is incentivized to come up with the ruleset that maximizes long-term researcher productivity. So if tenure really does work better than constant vicious competition, then (absent the usual culprits like resistance-to-change, weird signaling equilibria, politics, etc) we should expect universities to converge on a tenure system in order to produce the best work. In fact, we should expect universities to evolve a really impressive ruleset for optimizing researcher incentives, just as impressive as the clever mechanisms the human body uses to prevent cancer (since this seems a bit optimistic, I assume the usual culprits are not absent).

The same is true for grant-writing; naively you would want some competition to make sure that only the best grant proposals get funded, but too much competition seems to stifle original research, so much so that some funders are throwing out the whole process and selecting grants by lottery[9], and others are running grants you can apply for in a half-hour and hear back about two days later[10]. If there's a feedback mechanism—if these different rulesets produce different-quality research, and grant programs that produce higher-quality research are more likely to get funded in the future—then the rulesets for grants will gradually evolve, and the competition for grants will take place in an environment with whatever the right evolutionary parameters for evolving good research are.

I don't want to say these things will definitely happen—you can read Inadequate Equilibria[11] for an idea of why not. But they *might*. The evolutionary dynamics which would normally prevent them can be overcome. Two-layer evolutionary systems can produce their own slack, if having slack would be a good idea.

IV.

That was a lot of paragraphs, and a lot of them started with "imagine a hypothetical situation where…". Let's look deeper into cases where an understanding of slack can inform how we think about real-world phenomena. Five examples:

1. Monopolies. Not the kind that survive off overregulation and patents, the kind that survive by being big enough to crush competitors. These are predators that exploit low-slack environments. If Boeing has a monopoly on building passenger planes, and is exploiting that by making shoddy products and overcharging consumers, then that means anyone else who built a giant airplane factory could make better products at a lower price, capture the whole airplane market, and become a zillionaire. Why don't they? Slack. In terms of those adaptive fitness landscapes, in between your current position (average Joe) and a much better position at the bottom of a deep pit (you own a giant airplane factor and are a zillionaire), there's a very big hill you have to climb—the part where you build Giant Airplane Factory Part 1, Giant Airplane Factory Part 2, etc. At each point in this hill, you are worse off than somebody who was not building an as-yet-unprofitable giant airplane factory. If you have infinite slack (maybe you are Jeff Bezos, have unlimited money, and will never go bankrupt no matter how much time and cost it takes before you start earning profits) you're fine. If you have more limited slack, your slack will run out and you'll be outcompeted before you make it to the greater-fitness deep pit.

Real monopolies are more complicated than this, because Boeing can shape up and cut prices when you're halfway to building your giant airplane factory, thus removing your incentive. Or they can do *actually* shady stuff. But none of this would matter if you already had your giant airplane factory fully built and ready to go—at worst, you and

Boeing would then be in a fair fight. Everything Boeing does to try to prevent you from building that factory is exploiting your slacklessness and trying to increase the height of that hill you have to climb before the really deep pit.

(Peter Thiel inverts the landscape metaphor and calls the hill a "moat", but he's getting at the same concept).

2. Tariffs. Same story. Here's the way I understand the history of the international auto industry—anyone who knows more can correct me if I'm wrong. Automobiles were invented in the early 20th century. Several Western countries developed homegrown auto industries more or less simultaneously, with the most impressive being Henry Ford's work on mass production in the US. Post-WWII Japan realized that its own auto industry would never be able to compete with more established Western companies, so it placed high tariffs on foreign cars, giving local companies like Nissan and Toyota a chance to get their act together. These companies, especially Toyota, invented a new form of auto production which was actually much more efficient than the usual American methods, and were eventually able to hold their own. They started exporting cars to the US; although American tariffs put them at a disadvantage, they were so much better than the American cars of the time that consumers preferred them anyway. After decades of losing out, the American companies adopted a more Japanese ethos, and were eventually able to compete on a level playing field again.

This is a story of things gone surprisingly *right*—Americans and Japanese alike were able to get excellent inexpensive cars. Two things had to happen for it to work. First, Japan had to have high enough tariffs to give their companies some slack—to let them develop their own homegrown methods from scratch without being immediately outcompeted by temporarily-superior American competitors. Second, America had to have low enough tariffs that eventually-superior

Japanese companies could outcompete American automakers, and Japan's fitness-improving innovations could spread.

From the perspective of a Toyota manager, this is analogous to the eyeless alien story. You start with some good-enough standard (blind animals, American car companies). You want to evolve a superior end product (eye-having animals, Toyota). The intermediate steps (an animal with only Eye Part 1, a kind of crappy car company that stumbles over itself trying out new things) are less fit than the good-enough standard. Only when the inferior intermediate steps are protected from competition (through evolutionary randomness, through tariffs) can the superior end product come into existence. But you want to keep enough competition that the superior end product can use its superiority to spread (there is enough evolutionary competition that having eyes reaches fixation, there is enough free trade that Americans preferentially buy Toyota and US car companies have to adopt its policies).

From the perspective of an economic historian, maybe it's a group selection story. The various stakeholders in the US auto industry— Ford, GM, suppliers, the government, labor, customers—competed with each other in a certain way and struck some compromise. The various stakeholders in the Japanese auto industry did the same. For some reason the American compromise worked worse than the Japanese one—I've heard stories about how US companies were more willing to defraud consumers for short-term profit, how US labor unions were more willing to demand concessions even at the cost of company efficiency, how regulators and executives were in bed with each other to the detriment of the product, etc. Every US interest group was acting in its own short-term self-interest, but the Japanese industry-as-a-whole outcompeted the American one and the Americans had to adjust.

3. Monopolies, Part II. Traditionally, monopolies have been among the most successful R&D centers. The most famous example is Xerox; it had a monopoly on photocopiers for a few decades before losing an antitrust suit in the late 1970s; during that period, its PARC R&D program invented "laser printing, Ethernet, the modern personal computer, graphical user interface (GUI) and desktop paradigm, object-oriented programming, [and] the mouse". The second most famous example is Bell Labs, which invented "radio astronomy, the transistor, the laser, the photovoltaic cell, the charge-coupled device, information theory, the Unix operating system, and the programming languages B, C, C++, and S" before the government broke up its parent company AT&T. Google seems to be trying something similar[12], though it's too soon to judge their outcomes.

These successes make sense. Research and development is a long-term gamble. Devoting more money to R&D decreases your near-term profits, but (hopefully) increases your future profits. Freed from competition, monopolies have limitless slack, and can afford to invest in projects that won't pay off for ten or twenty years. This is part of Peter Thiel's defense of monopolies in *Zero To One*.

An administrator tasked with advancing technology might be tempted to encourage monopolies in order to get more research done. But monopolies can also be stagnant and resistant to change; it's probably not a coincidence that Xerox wasn't the first company to bring the personal computer to market, and ended up irrelevant to the computing revolution. Like the eyeless aliens, who will not evolve in conditions of perfect competition or perfect lack of competition, probably all you can do here is strike a balance. Some Communist countries tried the extreme solution—one state-supported monopoly per industry—and it failed the test of group selection. I don't know enough to have an opinion on whether countries with strong antitrust eventually outcompete those with weaker antitrust or vice versa.

4. Strategy Games. I like the strategy game *Civilization*, where you play as a group of primitives setting out to found a empire. You build cities and infrastructure, research technologies, and fight wars. Your world is filled with several (usually 2 to 7) other civilizations trying to do the same.

Just like in the real world, civilizations must decide between Guns and Butter. The Civ version of Guns is called the Axe Rush. You immediately devote all your research to discovering how to make really good axes, all your industry to manufacturing those axes, and all your population into wielding those axes. Then you go and hack everyone else to pieces while they're still futzing about trying to invent pottery or something.

The Civ version of Butter is called Build. You devote all your research, industry, and populace to laying the foundations of a balanced economy and culture. You invent pottery and weaving and stuff like that. Soon you have a thriving trade network and a strong philosophical tradition. Eventually you can field larger and more advanced armies than your neighbors, and leverage the advantage into even more prosperity, or into military conquest.

Consider a very simple scenario: a map of Eurasia with two civilizations, Rome and China.

If both choose Axe Rush, then whoever Axe Rushes better wins.

If both choose Build, then whoever Builds better wins.

What if Rome chooses Axe Rush, and China chooses Build?

Then it depends on their distance! If it's a very small map and they start very close together, Rome will probably overwhelm the Chinese before Build starts paying off. But if it's a very big map, by the time Roman Axemen trek all the way to China, China will have Built high walls, discovered longbows and other defensive technologies, and generally become too strong for axes to defeat. Then they can crush the Romans—who are still just axe-wielding primitives—at their leisure.

Consider a more complicated scenario. You have a map of Earth. The Old World contains Rome and China. The New World contains Aztecs. Rome and China are very close to each other. Now what happens?

Rome and China spend the Stone, Bronze, and Iron Ages hacking each other to bits. Aztecs spend those Ages building cities, researching technologies, and building unique Wonders of the World that provide powerful bonuses. In 1492, they discover Galleons and start crossing the ocean. The powerful and advanced Aztec empire crushes the exhausted axe-wielding Romans and Chinese.

This is another story about slack. The Aztecs had it—they were under no competitive pressure to do things that paid off next turn. The Romans and Chinese didn't—they had to be at the top of their game every single turn, or their neighbor would conquer them. If there was an option that made you 10% weaker next turn in exchange for making you 100% stronger ten turns down the line, the Aztecs could take it without a second thought; the Romans and Chinese would probably have to pass.

Okay, more complicated *Civilization* scenario. This time there are two Old World civs, Rome and China, and two New World civs, Aztecs and Inca. The map is stretched a little bit so that all four civilizations have the same amount of natural territory. All four players understand the map layout and can communicate with each other. What happens?

Now it's a group selection problem. A skillful Rome player will private message the China player and explain all of this to her. She'll remind him that if one hemisphere spends the whole Stone Age fighting, and the other spends it building, the builders will win. She might tell him that she knows the Aztec and Inca players, they're smart, and they're going to be discussing the same considerations. So it would benefit both Rome and China to sign a peace treaty dividing the Old World in two, stick to their own side, and Build. If both sides cooperate, they'll both Build strong empires capable of matching the New World players. If one side cooperates and the other defects, it will easily steamroll over its unprepared opponent and conquer the whole Old World. If both sides defect, they'll hack each other to death with axes and be easy prey for the New Worlders.

This might be true in *Civilization* games, but real-world civilizations are more complicated. Graham Greene wrote:

In Italy, for thirty years under the Borgias, they had warfare, terror, murder and bloodshed, but they produced Michelangelo, Leonardo da Vinci and the Renaissance. In Switzerland, they had brotherly love, they had five hundred years of democracy and peace—and what did that produce? The cuckoo clock.

So maybe a little bit of internal conflict is good, to keep you honest. Too much conflict, and you tear yourselves apart and are easy prey for outsiders. Too little conflict, and you invent the cuckoo clock and nothing else. The continent that conquers the world will have enough pressure that its people want to innovate, *and* enough slack that they're able to.

This is total ungrounded amateur historical speculation, but when I hear that I think of the Classical world. We can imagine it as divided into a certain number of "theaters of civilization"—Greece,

Mesopotamia, Egypt, Persia, India, Scythia, etc. Each theater had its own rules governing average state size, the rules of engagement between states, how often bigger states conquered smaller states, how often ideas spread between states of the same size, etc. Some of those theaters were intensely competitive: Egypt was a nice straight line, very suited to centralized rule. Others had more slack: it was really hard to take over all of Greece; even the Spartans didn't manage. Each theater conducted its own "evolution" in its own way—Egypt was ruled by a single Pharaoh without much competition, Scythia was constant warfare of all against all, Greece was isolated city-states that fought each other sometimes but also had enough slack to develop philosophy and science. Each of those systems did their own thing for a while, until finally one of them produced something perfect: 4th century BC Macedonia. Then it went out and conquered everything.

If Greene is right, the point isn't to find the ruleset that promotes 100% cooperation. It's to find the ruleset that promotes an evolutionary system that makes your group the strongest. Usually this involves some amount of competition—in order to select for stronger organisms—but also some amount of slack—to let organisms develop complicated strategies that can make them stronger. Despite the earlier description, this isn't necessarily a slider between 0% competition and 100% competition. It could be much more complicated—maybe alternating high-slack vs. low-slack periods, or many semi-isolated populations with a small chance of interaction each generation, or alternation between periods of isolation and periods of churning.

In a full two-layer evolution, you would let the systems evolve until they reached the best parameters. Here we can't do that—Greece has however many mountains it has; its success does not cause the rest of the world to grow more mountains. Still, we randomly started with enough different groups that we got to learn something interesting.

(I can't emphasize enough how ungrounded this historical speculation is. Please don't try to evolve Alexander the Great in your basement and then get angry at me when it doesn't work)

5. The Long-Term Stock Exchange. Actually, all stock exchanges are about slack. Imagine you are a brilliant inventor who, given $10 million and ten years, could invent fusion power. But in fact you have $10 and need work tomorrow or you will starve. Given those constraints, maybe you could start, I don't know, a lemonade stand.

You're in the same position as the animal trying to evolve an eye—you could create something very high-utility, if only you had enough slack to make it happen. But by default, the inventor working on fusion power starves to death ten days from now (or at least makes less money than his counterpart who ran the lemonade stand), the same way the animal who evolves Eye Part 1 gets outcompeted by other animals who didn't and dies out.

You need slack. In the evolution example, animals usually stumble across slack randomly. You too might stumble across slack randomly—maybe it so happens that you are independently wealthy, or won the lottery, or something.

More likely, you use the investment system. You ask rich people to give you $10 million for ten years so you can invent fusion; once you do, you'll make trillions of dollars and share some of it with them.

This is a great system. There's no evolutionary equivalent. An animal can't pitch Darwin on its three-step plan to evolve eyes and get free food and mating opportunities to make it happen. Wall Street is a giant multi-trillion dollar time machine funneling future profits back into the past, and that gives people the slack they need to make the future profits happen at all.

But the Long-Term Stock Exchange[13] is especially about slack. They are a new exchange (approved by the SEC last year) which has complicated rules about who can list with them. Investors will get extra clout by agreeing to hold stocks for a long time; executives will get incentivized to do well in the far future instead of at the next quarterly earnings report. It's making a deliberate choice to give companies more slack than the regular system and see what they do with it. I don't know enough about investing to have an opinion, except that I appreciate the experiment. Presumably its companies will do better/worse than companies on the regular stock exchange, that will cause companies to flock toward/away from it, and we'll learn that its new ruleset is better/worse at evolving good companies through competition than the regular stock exchange's ruleset.

6. That Time Ayn Rand Destroyed Sears. Or at least that's how Michael Rozworski and Leigh Phillips describe Eddie Lampert's corporate reorganization in How Ayn Rand Destroyed Sears[14], which I recommend. Lampert was a Sears CEO who figured—since free-market competitive economies outcompete top-down economies, shouldn't free-market competitive companies outcompete top-down companies? He reorganized Sears as a set of competing departments that traded with each other on normal free-market principles; if the Product Department wanted its products marketed, it would have to pay the Marketing Department. This worked really badly, and was one of the main contributors to Sears' implosion.

I don't have a great understanding of exactly why Lampert's Sears lost to other companies, but capitalist economies beat socialist ones; Rozworski and Phillips' People's Republic Of Wal-Mart[15], which looks into this question, is somewhere on my reading list. But even without complete understanding, we can use group selection to evolve the right parameters. Imagine an economy with several businesses. One is a straw-man communist collective, where every worker gets paid the same regardless of output and there are no promotions (0% competition, 100% cooperation). Another is Lampert's Sears (100% competition, 0% cooperation). Others are normal businesses, where employees mostly work together for the good of the company but also compete for promotions (X% competition, Y% cooperation). Presumably the normal business outcompetes both Lampert and the commies, and we sigh with relief and continue having normal businesses. And if some of the normal businesses outcompete others, we've learned something about the best values of X and Y.

7. Ideas. These are in constant evolutionary competition—this is the insight behind memetics[16]. The memetic equivalent of slack is inferential range, aka "willingness to entertain and explore ideas before deciding that they are wrong".

Inferential distance[17] is the number of steps it takes to make someone understand and accept a certain idea. Sometimes inferential distances can be very far apart. Imagine trying to convince a 12th century monk that there was no historical Exodus from Egypt. You're in the middle of going over archaeological evidence when he objects that the Bible says there was. You respond that the Bible is false and there's no God. He says that doesn't make sense, how would life have originated? You say it evolved from single-celled organisms. He asks how evolution, which seems to be a change in animals' accidents, could ever affect their essences and change them into an entirely new species. You say that the whole scholastic worldview is wrong, there's no such thing as accidents and essences, it's just atoms and empty space. He asks how you ground morality if not in a striving to approximate the ideal embodied by your essence, you say…well, it doesn't matter what you say, because you were trying to convince him that some very specific people didn't leave Egypt one time, and now you've got to ground morality.

Another way of thinking about this is that there are two self-consistent equilibria. There's your equilibrium, (no Exodus, atheism, evolution, atomism, moral nonrealism), and the monk's equilibrium (yes Exodus, theism, creationism, scholasticism, teleology), and before you can make the monk budge on any of those points, you have to convince him of all of them.

So the question becomes—how much patience does this monk have? If you tell him there's no God, does he say "I look forward to the several years of careful study of your scientific and philosophical theories that it will take for that statement not to seem obviously wrong and contradicted by every other feature of the world"? Or does he say "KILL THE UNBELIEVER"? This is inferential range.

Aristotle says that the mark of an educated man is to be able to entertain an idea without accepting it. Inferential range explains why. The monk certainly shouldn't immediately accept your claim, when he has countless pieces of evidence for the existence of God, from the spectacular faith healings he has witnessed ("look, there's this thing called psychosomatic illness, and it's really susceptible to this other thing called the placebo effect…") to Constantine's victory at the Milvian Bridge despite being heavily outnumbered ("look, I'm not a classical scholar, but some people are just really good generals and get lucky, and sometimes it happens the day after they have weird dreams, I think there's enough good evidence the other way that this is not the sort of thing you should center your worldview around"). But if he's willing to entertain your claim long enough to hear your arguments one by one, eventually he can reach the same self-consistent equilibrium you're at and judge for himself.

Nowadays we don't burn people at the stake. But we do make fun of them, or flame them, or block them, or wander off, or otherwise not listen with an open mind to ideas that strike us at first as stupid. This is another case where we have to balance competition vs. slack. With perfect competition, the monk instantly rejects our "no Exodus" idea as less true (less memetically fit) than its competitors, and it has no chance to grow on him. With zero competition, the monk doesn't believe anything at all, or spends hours patiently listening to someone explain their world-is-flat theory. Good epistemics require a balance between being willing to choose better ideas over worse ones, and open-mindedly hearing the worse ones out in case they grow on you.

(Thomas Kuhn[18] points out that early versions of the heliocentric model were much worse than the geocentric model, that astronomers only kept working on them out of a sort of weird curiosity, and that it took decades before they could clearly hold their own against geocentrism in a debate).

Different people strike a different balance in this space, and those different people succeed or fail based on their own epistemic ruleset. Someone who's completely closed-minded and dogmatic probably won't succeed in business, or science, or the military, or any other career (except maybe politics). But someone who's so pathologically open-minded that they listen to everything and refuse to prioritize what is or isn't worth their time will also fail. We take notice of who succeeds or fails and change our behavior accordingly.

Maybe there's even a third layer of selection; maybe different communities are more or less willing to tolerate open-minded vs. close-minded people. The Slate Star Codex community has really different epistemics norms from the Catholic Church or Infowars listeners; these are evolutionary parameters that determine which ideas are more memetically fit. If our epistemics make us more likely to converge on useful (not necessarily true!) ideas, we will succeed and our epistemic norms will catch on. Francis Bacon was just some guy with really good epistemic norms, and now everybody who wants to be taken seriously has to use his norms instead of whatever they were doing before. Come up with the right evolutionary parameters, and that could be you!

Endnotes

(1) Jerry A. Coyne. Why Evolution is True. Jan 2009

(2) Wikipedia. Whale fall.

(3) Scott Alexander. Meditations on Moloch. 30th Jul 2014.

(4) Zvi Mowshowitz. Slack. 30th Sep 2017.

(5) Wikipedia. Lotka—Volterra equations.

(6) Scott Alexander. Book Review: Secular Cycles. 12th Aug 2019.

(7) Eliezer Yudkowsky. The Tragedy of Group Selectionism. 6th Nov 2007.

(8) Scott Alexander. The Goddess of Everything Else. 17th Au 2015.

(9) Kelsey Piper. Science funding is a mess. Could grant lotteries make it better?. 18th Jan 2019.

(10) Kelsey Piper. This new charity offers scientists coronavirus grants in 48 hours. 21st Apr 2020

(11) Scott Alexander. Book Review: Inadequate Equilibria. 30th Nov 2017.

(12) Wikipedia. X Development.

(13) Theodore Schleifer. America's newest stock exchange wants to fix one of capitalism's fundamental challenges. 22nd May 2019.

(14) Michael Rozworski & Leigh Phillips. Failing to Plan: How Ayn Rand Destroyed Sears. 18th Juy 2019.

(15) Michael Rozworski & Leigh Phillips. The People's Republic of Walmart: How the World's Biggest Corporations are Laying the Foundation for Socialism. 5th Mar 2019.

(16) Wikipedia. Memetics.

(17) Eliezer Yudkowsky. Expecting Short Inferential Distances. 22nd Oct 2007.

(18) Scott Alexander. Book Review: The Structure of Scientific Revolutions. 8th Jan 2019.

Elizabeth Van Nostrand, Jim Babcock

Credibility of the CDC on SARS-CoV-2

Editor's note: This post was originally published on March 6 2020, and played an important role in how the LessWrong community evaluated information during the pandemic.

Introduction

One of the main places Americans look for information on coronavirus is the Center for Disease Control and Prevention (abbreviated CDC from the days before "and Prevention" was in the title). That's natural; "handling contagious epidemics" is not their only job, but it is one of their primary ones, and they position themselves as the authority. At a time when so many things are uncertain, it saves a lot of anxiety (and time, and money) to have an expert source you can turn to and get solid advice.

Unfortunately, the CDC has repeatedly given advice with lots of evidence against it. Below is a list of actions from the CDC that we believe are misleading or otherwise indicative of an underlying problem.

Examples

Dismissed Risk of Infection Via Packages

On the CDC's coronavirus FAQs pages on 2020-03-04,[1] they say, under "Am I at risk for COVID-19 from a package or products shipping from China?":

"In general, because of poor survivability of these coronaviruses on surfaces, there is likely very low risk of spread from products or packaging that are shipped over a period of days or weeks at ambient temperatures."

However, this meta review[2] found that various coronaviruses remained infectious for days at room temperature on certain surfaces (cardboard was not tested, alas) and potentially weeks at lower temperatures. The CDC's answer is probably correct for packages *from China*, and it's possible it's even right for domestic packages with 2-day shipping, but it is incorrect to say that coronaviruses in general have low survivability, and to the best of my ability to determine, we don't have the experiments that would prove deliveries are safe.

Blinded Itself to Community Spread

As late as 2020-02-29, the CDC was reporting that there had been no "community spread" of SARS-CoV-2. (Community spread means that the person hadn't been traveling in an infected area or associating with someone who had). At this time, the CDC would only test a person for SARS-CoV-2 if they had been in China or in close contact with a confirmed COVID-19 case.[3]

Clinical Features	&	Epidemiologic Risk
Fever or signs/symptoms of lower respiratory illness (e.g. cough or shortness or breath)	AND	Any person, including health care workers, who has had close contact with a laboratory-confirmed 2019-nCoV patient within 14 days of symptom onset
Fever and signs/symptoms of a lower respiratory illness (e.g., cough or shortness of breath)	AND	A history of travel from Hubei Province, China within 14 days of symptom onset
Fever and signs/symptoms of a lower respiratory illness (e.g., cough or shortness of breath) requiring hospitalization	AND	A history of travel from mainland China within 14 days of symptom onset

Testing Criteria as of 2020-02-11[4]

This not only left them incapable of detecting community spread, it ignored potential cases who had travelled to other countries with known COVID-19 outbreaks.

By 2020-02-13,[5] this had been amended to include:

"The criteria are intended to serve as guidance for evaluation. Patients should be evaluated and discussed with public health departments on a case-by-case basis. For severely ill individuals, testing can be considered when exposure history is equivocal (e.g., uncertain travel or exposure, or no known exposure) and another etiology has not been identified."

(The CDC describes this change as happening on 2020-02-12, however the Wayback Machine did not capture the page that day).

Based on this announcement on 2020-02-14,[6] when testing that could detect community exposure was happening it was in one of 5 major cities. However as of 2020-03-01[7] only 472 tests had been done, so no test could have been happening very often.

Between 2020-02-27 and 2020-02-28, the primary guidelines on this page were amended to:

Clinical Features	&	Epidemiologic Risk
Fever or signs/symptoms of lower respiratory illness (e.g. cough or shortness or breath)	AND	Any person, including health care workers, who has had close contact with a laboratory-confirmed COVID-19 patient within 14 days of symptom onset
Fever and signs/symptoms of a lower respiratory illness (e.g., cough or shortness of breath) requiring hospitalization	AND	A history of travel from affected geographic areas (see below) within 14 days of symptom onset
Fever with severe acute lower respiratory illness (e.g., pneumonia, ARDS) requiring hospitalization and without alternative explanatory diagnosis (e.g., influenza)	AND	No source of exposure has been identified

However guidance went out on the same day (the 28th) that only listed China as a risk (and even then, only medium risk unless they had been exposed to a confirmed case or travelled to Hubei specifically).

Testing Kits the CDC Sent to Local Labs were Unreliable

They generated too many false positives to be useful.[8]

Hamstrung Detection by Banning 3rd Party Testing (HHS/FDA, not CDC)

One reason the CDC used such stringent criteria for determining who to test was that they had a very limited ability to test, hamstrung further by the faulty tests sent to local labs. Normally private testing would fill the gap, but the department of Health and Human Services invoked emergency measures that created a requirement for special approval of tests, and the FDA didn't grant it to anyone (source[9]).

There are multiple harrowing stories of people with obvious symptoms and exposure to the virus being turned away from testing, often against a doctor's pleas:

- UC Davis patient[10]

- NYC ER doctor complains about inability to test[11]

- NYC man returning from Japan[12]

- Northern California nurse who treated infected patient[13]

There is also a rumor[14] that the first case caught in Seattle, which has since turned into the US epicenter of the disease, was caught by a research lab using a loophole to perform unauthorized testing (raising the possibility that it's worse elsewhere and simply hasn't been caught).

Ceased to Report Number of Tests Run

Until 2020-03-02, the CDC reported how many tests SARS-CoV-2 tests it had run. On March 2nd, it stopped (before,[15] after[16]). There are many potential reasons for this, none of which inspire confidence. The official reason for this as told to[17] reporter Kelsey Piper is that the number would no longer be representative now that states are running their own tests. So, best case scenario, the CDC can not coordinate enough to count tests performed by other labs.

Gave False Reassurances About Recovered Individuals

As of this writing (2020-03-05[18]), the CDC's "Share Facts" page states that "Someone who has completed quarantine or has been released from isolation does not pose a risk of infection to other people."

While it is certainly true that being released from quarantine implies a significantly reduced risk, the quarantine that is typically performed is not stringent enough to say that people released pose no risk. The quarantine procedure performed by the CDC[19] lasts 14 days, after which if symptoms have not appeared, they can be released.

There are case reports of individuals with incubation periods of 27 days[20] and 19 days.[21] There was a case in Texas where a person tested positive after being released from quarantine and visiting a mall.[22]

While an epidemic is still contained, safely quarantining at-risk people means choosing a quarantine period long enough to be confident that, if they haven't shown symptoms, they don't have the disease. When a disease is still contained, this should be risk averse, since a single infected person could start an outbreak. The CDC's 14-day quarantine period was not long enough to catch the cases detailed above.

This was foreseeable. This paper,[23] published Feb 6 and reproduced in the table, opposite, estimated the distribution of incubation periods, including the incubation periods of outliers.

	Incubation period distribution (days)					
Percentiles	Weibull		Gamma		Lognormal	
	Estimate	95% CI	Estimate	95% CI	Estimate	95% CI
2.5th	2.1	1.3-3.0	2.4	1.5-3.2	2.4	1.6-3.1
5th	2.7	1.8-3.5	2.9	2.0-3.6	2.8	2.0-3.5
50th	6.4	5.5-7.5	6.1	5.3-7.3	6.1	5.2-7.4
95th	10.3	8.6-14.1	11.3	9.1-15.7	13.3	9.9-20.5
97.5th	11.1	9.1-15.5	12.5	9.9-17.9	15.5	11.0-25.2
99th	11.9	9.7-17.2	14.1	10.9-20.6	18.5	12.6-32.3

The relevant row is the 99th percentile row, which estimates the longest incubation period per 100 people. If you quarantined 100 people, one of them would have an incubation period at least that long. The paper estimates this using three different methods; two of

Elizabeth Van Nostrand, Jim Babcock

those estimates are greater than 14 days, and all three estimates put significant probability on incubation periods longer than 14 days.

There are also reports[24] of the virus re-emerging in patients who were believed to have recovered.

Conflated Genetics and Environmental Exposure

This is a tough topic to write about.

Cruelty to people because they have or might have a disease is never okay. And the vast majority of people who were cruel to Asian-appearing people in the early days of an epidemic were doing it to healthy people out of knee jerk fear and antagonism, not a measured, well-informed cost-benefit analysis. When the CDC claimed on 2020-02-29[25] that "People of Asian descent, including Chinese Americans, are not more likely to get COVID-19 than any other American." they were surely trying to dampen attacks on people who had done nothing wrong and were hurting no one.

But the statement is false. Chinese-Americans are more likely to travel to China or associate with people who have, and thus were more likely to catch SARS-CoV-2. This doesn't mean they are more likely to catch it *given exposure*, but they were more likely to be exposed.

The CDC admits this in the page specifically on stigma (2020-02-24[26]), saying "People—including those of Asian descent—who have not recently traveled to China or been in contact with a person who is a confirmed or suspected case of COVID-19 are not at greater risk of acquiring and spreading COVID-19 than other Americans."

However, that same anti-stigma page goes on to say "Viruses cannot target people from specific populations, ethnicities, or racial backgrounds." This is also false. About 10% of Europeans are immune to HIV,[27] an immunity not found people originating from other areas. So we know it is technically possible for a virus to have differential effects based on race.

Does SARS-CoV-2 in particular have race-related effects? There are people claiming Asian men are more susceptible to SARS-CoV-2 than others due to a higher expression of a certain protein (example[28]). Other people dispute this (example[29]). Right now it is very much an open question.

We can see why the CDC prioritized calming racially-motivated violence over fully explaining their confusion over an unanswered question. It might have been the highest-utility thing to do. But it is important to know that "misrepresenting data in order to produce better actions from the public" is a thing the CDC does.

Discouraged Use of Masks

Which brings us to the CDC's statement on masks:[30]

CDC does not recommend that people who are well wear a facemask to protect themselves from respiratory diseases, including COVID-19.

The Surgeon General (who is not directly part of the CDC) takes a stronger tack:

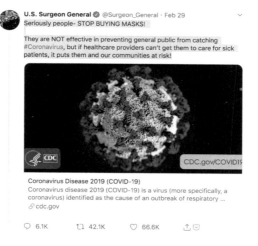

U.S. Surgeon General @ @Surgeon_General · Feb 29
Seriously people- STOP BUYING MASKS!

They are NOT effective in preventing general public from catching #Coronavirus, but if healthcare providers can't get them to care for sick patients, it puts them and our communities at risk!

Coronavirus Disease 2019 (COVID-19)
Coronavirus disease 2019 (COVID-19) is a virus (more specifically, a coronavirus) identified as the cause of an outbreak of respiratory ...
🔗 cdc.gov

💬 6.1K   🔁 42.1K   ♡ 66.6K   ⬆️ ♡

While we can't hold the CDC responsible for the Surgeon General, they are being conflated in a lot of news articles saying or implying that masks are useless for healthy people. They're (probably) not.

Our best guess is that the CDC is trying to conserve masks for health care professionals and others with the highest need, in the face of a looming mask shortage. That could easily be the optimum mask allocation. I can't prove the lie wasn't justified for the greater good. But it is another example of the CDC placing "getting the outcome it wants" over "telling people the literal truth."

What Does This Mean?

These errors we've highlighted tend towards errors of omission: saying something is completely safe when it's not, saying something is unhelpful when it is, saying the current state is less dangerous than it is. You should include that bias when processing new information from the CDC. Notably **we're not saying any of the things they do recommend are bad**: to the best of our knowledge, you should be washing your hands and not touching your face. Vaccines are (mostly) great. But I would not take the CDC saying an activity is safe or unnecessary as the last word on the subject.

Endnotes

(1) https://web.archive.org/web/20200304001555/https://www.cdc.gov/coronavirus/2019-ncov/faq.html

(2) https://www.ncbi.nlm.nih.gov/pubmed/14631830

(3) https://twitter.com/ScottGottliebMD/status/1224043385960435713

(4) https://web.archive.org/web/20200211025718/https://www.cdc.gov/coronavirus/2019-ncov/hcp/clinical-criteria.html

(5) https://web.archive.org/web/20200213123640/https://www.cdc.gov/coronavirus/2019-ncov/hcp/clinical-criteria.html

(6) https://web.archive.org/web/20200215132532/https://www.cdc.gov/media/releases/2020/t0214-covid-19-update.html.html

(7) https://twitter.com/JuddLegum/status/1234536619270688768/photo/1

(8) https://www.propublica.org/article/cdc-coronavirus-covid-19-test?fbclid=IwAR2YbEiC-KqaofziCF2-W6ibnD0qrH1ChI-yg4WR6DlGhcIcZ5v4F_-kGaFE

(9) https://twitter.com/ScottGottliebMD/status/1224042220665307137

(10) https://thehill.com/policy/healthcare/484903-cdc-declined-to-test-new-coronavirus-patient-for-days-california-hospital

(11) https://www.cnbc.com/amp/2020/03/02/coronavirus-new-york-

city-doctor-has-to-plead-to-test-people.html

(12) https://www.businessinsider.com/new-york-man-denied-corona-virus-test-japan-trip-fever-cough-2020-3

(13) https://act.nationalnursesunited.org/page/-/files/graphics/NU-Quarantine-RN-press-conf-statement.pdf

(14) https://www.statnews.com/2020/03/03/washing-ton-state-risks-seeing-explosion-in-coronavirus-without-dramatic-ac-tion-new-analysis-says/

(15) https://web.archive.org/web/20200302100135/https://www.cdc.gov/coronavirus/2019-ncov/cases-in-us.html

(16) https://web.archive.org/web/20200302222137/https://www.cdc.gov/coronavirus/2019-ncov/cases-in-us.html

(17) https://twitter.com/KelseyTuoc/status/1234872230426755073

(18) https://web.archive.org/web/20200305134343/https://www.cdc.gov/coronavirus/2019-ncov/about/share-facts.html

(19) https://web.archive.org/web/20200305183724/https://www.cdc.gov/mmwr/volumes/69/wr/mm6909e1.htm?s_cid=mm6909e1_w

(20) https://www.reuters.com/article/us-china-health-incubation/coronavirus-incubation-could-be-as-long-as-27-days-chinese-provin-cial-government-says-idUSKCN20G06W

(21) https://jamanetwork.com/journals/jama/fullarticle/2762028

(22) https://www.cnbc.com/2020/03/02/cdc-released-a-wom-

an-in-texas-who-tested-positive-for-the-coronavirus-totally-unaccept-
able.html

(23) https://www.eurosurveillance.org/content/10.2807/1560-7917.
ES.2020.25.5.2000062

(24) https://www.reuters.com/article/us-china-health-reinfection-ex-
plainer/explainer-coronavirus-reappears-in-discharged-patients-rai-
sing-questions-in-containment-fight-idUSKCN20M124?utm_
source=reddit.com

(25) https://web.archive.org/web/20200229164715/https://www.
cdc.gov/coronavirus/2019-ncov/about/share-facts.html

(26) https://web.archive.org/web/20200224023250/https://www.
cdc.gov/coronavirus/2019-ncov/about/related-stigma.html

(27) https://www.sciencedaily.com/releases/2005/03/050325234239.
htm

(28) https://www.nature.com/articles/s41421-020-0147-1?fbclid=I-
wAR1mwnPnSrcXLLselhmsCWB58nsxt9sy6nCojrHlvxGx2Su8_
Owy1HCgSsQ

(29) https://www.preprints.org/manuscript/202002.0258/v1/down-
load

(30) https://web.archive.org/web/20200303041220/https://www.
cdc.gov/coronavirus/2019-ncov/about/prevention-treatment.html

"Can you keep this confidential? How do you know?"

P et peeve about privacy: I think people are woefully inadequate at asking, and answering, "Can you keep this confidential?"

Disclosure: I am not inherently great at keeping information private. By default, if a topic came up in conversation, I would accidentally sometimes say my thoughts before I had time to realize "oh, right, this was private information I shouldn't share."

I've worked over the past few years to become better at this—I've learned several specific skills and habits that make it easier. But I didn't learn those skills in school, and no one even really suggested I was supposed to learn them. People seemed to just assume "People can keep secrets, and it's low cost for them to do so."

And... maybe this is just me. But, people say to me, "Hey, can you keep this private?", in a tone that implies I'm not really supposed to say no. And that's the *best* case. I've also observed things like...

...people saying "Hey, this is confidential", and then just saying the thing without checking in.

...people saying "Sign this NDA", without really checking I have the skills to honor that agreement, and if I were to *not* sign, I'd... probably get fired? Unclear.

...people gathering for a Circle* or other private safe space, and saying (best case) "Do we all agree to keep things here confidential? Raise your hand?" and worst case, just flatly asserting "This is a safe space, things are confidential here". (And I have seen at least one instance where someone I actively trusted later betrayed that trust.)

...people saying "You can report things to our [org / HR department / point-person], and they will keep things confidential." But, I know that in the hiring process for that org or department, no one ever checked that people actually had privacy skills.

---

* Circling is a group "meditative", "relational" practice. Typically, a group of people sit in a circle and deliberately focus their attention the emotions and experiences of each participant in the group. Communication is usually restricted to the topic of what the individuals in the Circle are experiencing in the present moment, particular their attitudes, feelings, and reactions to others in the group.

And meanwhile, I have almost never heard anyone say something like "I have been given 10 bits of private-info over the past few years, and I accidentally leaked two of them", or even "I have paid any attention at all to how leaky I am with regards to confidential information."

What is a secret, even?

Meanwhile, people seem to vary in what they even mean by "secret" or "private information". Some people take them as serious oaths, some people just kinda sorta try to keep the R^0 of the info lower than 1. Sometimes it seems to mean "carry this information to your grave", and sometimes it means "I dunno keep this on the down-low for awhile until the current controversy blows over".

Some people reading this might be surprised this is even a big deal. I gave a lightning-talk version of this essay in 2020, and one person asked, "Does this really matter that much, outside of major company NDAs or state-secrets?" Another person expressed similar skepticism.

I think it varies. The problem is exactly that *most* of the time, secrets aren't that big of a deal. But people don't seem to take time to get on the same page of exactly how big a deal they are, which is a recipe for mismatched expectations.

It's a bigger deal for me, because I live in social and professional circles adjacent to EA Grantmaking where the line between the personal and professional is (perhaps unfortunately) a bit blurry. Sometimes, I talk to people exploring ideas that are legit infohazardous. Sometimes, people are hesitant to talk because they're worried it may affect their career.

It's also important to me from a Robust Agency₁ standpoint—I'd like to be a reliable agent that people can coordinate with in complicated domains. Many other people in the x-risk ecosystem also seem interested in that. I think "the ability to exchange information, or reliably not exchange it" is a key skill, and worth cultivating because it enables higher-order strategies.

What to do with all this?

I don't have a clear next action with all this. Right now, there's a vague social norm that you're supposed to be able to keep secrets, and that certain types of information tend to be private-by-default, but outside of things like "your social security number", there's not much agreement on *what*.

What I've personally taken to doing is giving myself a TAP*, where as soon as I notice that a conversation or relationship is moving in the direction where someone might want to give me private information (or vice versa), I say, "Hey, I'd like to have a little meta-discussion about privacy".

And then we have a chat. If the conversation literally *just* broached the idea that one of us share private info, I try to avoid face-to-face contact to avoid micro-expressions revealing information. (Someone else recently suggested leaving more pauses in the conversation, so that reaction-time doesn't reveal information either).

---

* Trigger-Action Planning (TAP), sometimes Trigger-Action Patterns, and formerly Implementation Intentions are techniques for getting oneself to successfully enact desired actions (or inactions) by training something like a "stimulus-response" pair. The technique was spread by CFAR which initially drew upon the psychology literature of Implementation Intentions.
After it was clear that TAPs should be heavily applied to cognitive motions/thought patterns, some decided that the "P" should stand for 'Pattern' rather than "Plan".

Then, I ask some questions like:

Can you keep a secret?

How do you know?

What exactly do you mean by secret?

Meanwhile, acknowledging: "Hey, so, in the past few years I've leaked at least one important bit of private-info. I haven't kept track of how much private info I *didn't* leak. But, I've also been working on gaining skills that make me more reliable at keeping things private, and making it lower cost for myself to take on confidential information. I'm fairly confident I can keep things private if I have to, but it's still a moderate cost to myself and I have to choose to do it on purpose. So please don't assume I'm keeping anything private unless I've specifically told you so."

I think it'd be good if such meta-conversations became more common.

I think they most importantly should be common if you are *creating an organization* that relies a lot on confidentiality. If you're promising to your clients that their information is private, but you aren't actually checking that your employees can keep confidence, you're creating integrity debt for yourself. You will need to pay it down sooner or later.

Endnotes

(1) Raymond Arnold. Being a Robust Agent. October 2018.

Abram Denski

Most Prisoner's Dilemmas are Stag Hunts; Most Stag Hunts are Schelling Problems

I previously claimed that most apparent Prisoner's Dilemmas are actually Stag Hunts. I now claim that they're Schelling Pub Games in practice. I conclude with some lessons for fighting Moloch.

This essay turned out especially dense with inferential leaps and unexplained terminology. Some ideas here are drawn from the work of Tsvi Benson-Tilsen.

The title of this essay used to be *Most Prisoner's Dilemmas are Stag Hunts; Most Stag Hunts are Battle of the Sexes*. I'm changing it based on this comment[1]. "Battle of the Sexes" is a game where a male and female (let's say Bob and Alice) want to hang out, but each of them would prefer to engage in gender-stereotyped behavior. For example, Bob wants to go to a football game, and Alice wants to go to a museum. The gender issues are distracting, and although it's the standard, *the game isn't that well-known anyway,* so sticking to the standard didn't buy me much (in terms of reader understanding).

I therefore present to you:

The Schelling Pub Game

Two friends would like to meet at the pub. In order to do so, they must make the same selection of pub (making this a Schelling-point game). However, they have different preferences about which pub to meet at. For example:

- Alice and Bob would both like to go to a pub this evening.

- There are two pubs: the Xavier, and the Yggdrasil.

- Alice likes the Xavier twice as much as the Yggdrasil.

- Bob likes the Yggdrasil twice as much as the Xavier.

- However, Alice and Bob also prefer to be with each other. Let's say they like being together ten times as much as they like being apart.

Schelling Pub Game payoff matrix

payoffs written alice; bob		B's choice	
		X	Y
A's choice	X	20;10	2;2
	Y	1;1	10;20

The important features of this game are:

- The Nash equilibria are all Pareto-optimal. There is no "individually rational agents work against each other" problem, like in prisoner's dilemma or even stag hunt.

- There are multiple equilibria, and different agents prefer different equilibria.

Thus, realistically, agents may not end up in equilibrium at all— because (in the single-shot game) they don't know which to choose, and because (in an iterated version of the game) they may make locally sub-optimal choices in order to influence the long-run behavior of other players.

(Edited to add, based on comments:)

Here's a summary of the central argument which, despite the lack of pictures, may be easier to understand.

1. Most Prisoner's Dilemmas (PDs) are actually iterated.

2. Iterated games are a whole different game with a different action space (because you can react to history), a different payoff matrix (because you care about future payoffs, not just the present), and a different set of equilibria.

3. It is characteristic of PD that players are incentivised to play away from the Pareto frontier; IE, no Pareto-optimal point is an equilibrium. This is not the case with iterated PD.

4. It is characteristic of Stag Hunt that there is a Pareto-optimal equilibrium, but there is also another equilibrium which is far from optimal. This is also the case with iterated PD. So **iterated PD resembles Stag Hunt.**

5. However, it is furthermore true of iterated PD that there are multiple different Pareto-optimal equilibria, which benefit different players more or less. Also, if players don't successfully coordinate on one of these equilibria, they can end up in a worse overall state (such as mutual defection forever, due to playing grim-trigger strategies with mutually incompatible demands). **This makes iterated PD resemble the Schelling Pub Game.**

In fact, the Folk Theorem suggests that most iterated games will resemble the Schelling Pub Game in this way.

In a comment[2] on The Schelling Choice is "Rabbit", not "Stag"[3], I said:

> In the book The Stag Hunt, Skyrms similarly says that lots of people use Prisoner's Dilemma to talk about

social coordination, and he thinks people should often use Stag Hunt instead.

I think this is right. Most problems which initially seem like Prisoner's Dilemma are actually Stag Hunt, because there are potential enforcement mechanisms available. The problems discussed in Meditations on Moloch are mostly Stag Hunt problems, not Prisoner's Dilemma problems—Scott even talks about enforcement, when he describes the dystopia where everyone has to kill anyone who doesn't enforce the terrible social norms (including the norm of enforcing).

This might initially sound like good news. Defection in a Prisoner's Dilemma is an inevitable conclusion under common decision-theoretic assumptions. Trying to escape multipolar traps with exotic decision theories might seem hopeless. On the other hand, Rabbit in a Stag Hunt is not an inevitable conclusion, by any means.

Unfortunately, in reality, hunting stag is actually quite difficult. ("The schelling choice is Rabbit, not Stag... and that really sucks!")

Inspired by Zvi Mowshowitz's recent sequence on Moloch[4], I wanted to expand on this. These issues are important, since they determine how we think about group action problems / tragedy of the commons / multipolar traps / Moloch / all the other synonyms for the same thing.

My current claim is that most Prisoner's Dilemmas are actually *Schelling pub games*. But let's first review the relevance of Stag Hunt.

Your PD Is Probably a Stag Hunt

There are several reasons why an apparent Prisoner's Dilemma may be more of a Stag Hunt.

- The game is actually an iterated game.

- Reputation networks could punish defectors and reward cooperators.

- There are enforceable contracts.

- Players know quite a bit about how other players think (in the extreme case, players can view each other's source code).

Each of these formal models creates a situation where players **can** get into a cooperative equilibrium. The challenge is that you can't unilaterally decide everyone should be in the cooperative equilibrium. If you want good outcomes for yourself, you have to account for what everyone else probably does. If you think everyone is likely to be in a bad equilibrium where people punish each other for cooperating, then aligning with that equilibrium might be the best you can do! This is like hunting rabbit.

Exercise: is there a situation in your life, or within spitting distance, which seems like a Prisoner's Dilemma to you, where everyone is stuck hurting each other due to bad incentives? Is it an iterated situation? Could there be reputation networks which weed out bad actors? Could contracts or contract-like mechanisms be used to encourage good behavior?

So, why do we perceive so many situations to be Prisoner's Dilemma -like rather than Stag Hunt -like? Why does Moloch sound more like *each individual is incentivized to make it worse for everyone else* than *everyone is stuck in a bad equilibrium?*

Sarah Constantin writes[5]:

> A friend of mine speculated that, in the decades that humanity has lived under the threat of nuclear war, we've developed the assumption that we're living in a world of one-shot Prisoner's Dilemmas rather than repeated games, and lost some of the social technology associated with repeated games. Game theorists do, of course, know about iterated games and there's some fascinating research in evolutionary game theory[6], but the original formalization of game theory was for the application of nuclear war, and the 101-level framing that most educated laymen hear is often that one-shot is the prototypical case and repeated games are hard to reason about without computer simulations.

To use board-game terminology, the *game* may be a Prisoner's Dilemma, but the *metagame* can use enforcement techniques. Accounting for enforcement techniques, the game is more like a Stag Hunt, where defecting is "rabbit" and cooperating is "stag".

Schelling Pubs

But this is a bit informal. You don't separately choose how to metagame and how to game; really, your iterated strategy determines what you do in individual games.

So it's more accurate to just think of the iterated game. There are a bunch of iterated strategies which you can choose from.

The key difference between the single-shot game and the iterated game is that cooperative strategies, such as Tit for Tat (but including[7] others[8]), are available. These strategies have the property that (1) they are equilibria—if you know the other player is playing Tit for Tat, there's no reason for you not to; (2) if both players use them, they end up cooperating.

A key feature of the Tit for Tat strategy is that if you do end up playing against a pure defector, you do almost as well as you could possibly do with them. This doesn't sound very much like a Stag Hunt. It begins to sound like a Stag Hunt in which you can change your mind and go hunt rabbit if the other person doesn't show up to hunt stag with you.

Sounds great, right? We can just play one of these cooperative strategies.

The problem is, there are many possible self-enforcing equilibria. Each player can threaten the other player with a *Grim Trigger* strategy: they defect forever the moment some specified condition isn't met. This can be used to extort the other player for more than just the mutual-cooperation payoff. Here's an illustration of possible outcomes, with the enforceable frequencies in the white area:

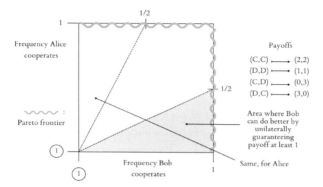

Payoffs

$(C,C) \longmapsto (2,2)$
$(D,D) \longmapsto (1,1)$
$(C,D) \longmapsto (0,3)$
$(D,C) \longmapsto (3,0)$

Area where Bob can do better by unilaterally guaranteeing payoff at least 1

Same, for Alice

Frequency Alice cooperates

$\sim\!\sim\!\sim$: Pareto frontier

Frequency Bob cooperates

The entire white area are enforceable equilibria: players could use a grim-trigger strategy to make each other cooperate with very close to the desired frequency, because what they're getting is still better than mutual defection, even if it is far from fair, or far from the Pareto frontier.

Alice could be extorting Bob by cooperating ⅔ of the time, with a grim-trigger threat of never cooperating at all. Alice would then get an average payoff of 2⅓, while Bob would get an average payout of 1⅓.

In the artificial setting of a Prisoner's Dilemma, it's easy to say that Cooperate, Cooperate is the "fair" solution, and an equilibrium like I just described is "Alice exploiting Bob". However, real games are not so symmetric, and so it will not be so obvious what "fair" is. The gray squiggle highlights the Pareto frontier—the space of outcomes which are "efficient" in the sense that no alternative is purely better for everybody. These outcomes may not all be fair, but they all have the advantage that no "money is left on the table"—any "improvement" we could propose for those outcomes makes things worse for at least one person.

Notice that I've also colored areas where Bob and Alice are doing worse than payoff 1. Bob can't enforce Alice's cooperation while defecting more than half the time; Alice would just defect. And vice versa. All of the points within the shaded regions have this property. So not *all* Pareto-optimal solutions can be enforced.

Any point in the white region can be enforced, however. Each player could be watching the statistics of the other player's cooperation, prepared to pull a grim-trigger if the statistics ever stray too far from the target point. This includes so-called **mutual blackmail** equilibria, in which both players cooperate with probability slightly better than zero (while threatening to never cooperate at all if the other player detectably diverges from that frequency). This idea—that "almost any" outcome can be enforced—is known as the Folk Theorem[9] in game theory.

The Schelling Pub part is that (particularly with grim-trigger enforcement) everyone has to choose the same equilibrium to enforce; otherwise everyone is stuck playing Defect. You'd even rather be in a bad mutual-blackmail type equilibrium, as opposed to selecting incompatible points to enforce. Just like in Schelling Pub, you'd prefer to meet together at any venue rather than end up at different places.

Furthermore, I would claim that *most* apparent Stag Hunts which you encounter in real life are actually Schelling Pub, in the sense that there are many different stags to hunt and it isn't immediately clear which one should be hunted. Each stag will be differently appealing to different people, so it's difficult to establish common knowledge[10] about which one is worth going after together.

Exercise: *which stags aren't you hunting with the people around you?*

Taking Pareto Improvements

Fortunately, Grim Trigger is not the *only* enforcement mechanism which can be used to build an equilibrium. Grim Trigger creates a crisis in which you've got to guess which equilibrium you're in very quickly, to avoid angering the other player; and no experimentation is allowed. There are much more forgiving[7] strategies (and contrite[8] ones, too, which helps in a different way).

Actually, *even using Grim Trigger to enforce things*, why would you punish the other player for doing something *better for you?* There's no motive for punishing the other player for raising their cooperation frequency.

In a scenario where you don't know which Grim Trigger the other player is using, but you don't think they'll punish you for cooperating *more* than the target, a natural response is for both players to just cooperate a bunch.

So, it can be very valuable to **use enforcement mechanisms which allow for Pareto improvements.**

Taking Pareto improvements is about moving from the middle to the boundary:

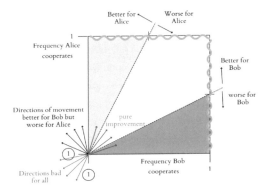

(I've indicated the directions for Pareto improvements starting from the origin in blue, as well as what happens in other directions; also, I drew a bunch of example Pareto improvements as light gray arrows in the white area to illustrate how Pareto improvements are awesome. Some of those arrows might not be perfectly within the range of Pareto improvements, sorry about that.)

However, there's also an argument against taking Pareto improvements. If you accept *any* Pareto improvements, you can be exploited in the sense mentioned earlier—you'll accept any situation, so long as it's not worse for you than where you started. So you will take some pretty poor deals. Notice that one Pareto improvement can prevent a different one—for example, if you move to ($\frac{1}{2}$, 1), then you can't move to (1,$\frac{1}{2}$) via Pareto improvement. So you could always reject a Pareto improvement because you're holding out for a better deal. (This is the *Schelling Pub* aspect of the situation—there are Pareto-optimal outcomes which are better or worse for different people, so it's hard to agree on which improvement to take.)

That's where Cooperation between Agents with Different Notions of Fairness[11] comes in. The idea in that post is that you don't take *just any* Pareto improvement—you have standards of fairness—but you don't just completely defect for less-than-perfectly-fair deals either. What this means is that two such agents with incompatible notions of fairness can't get all the way to the Pareto frontier, but the closer their notions of fairness are to each other, the closer they can get. And, if the notions of fairness *are* compatible, they can get all the way.

Moloch is the Folk Theorem

Because of the Folk Theorem, *most* iterated games will have the same properties I've been talking about (not just iterated PD). Specifically, most iterated games will have:

1. Stag-hunt-like property 1: There is a Pareto-optimal equilibrium, but there is also an equilibrium far from Pareto-optimal.

2. The Schelling Pub property: There are multiple Pareto-optimal equilibria, so that even if you're trying to cooperate, you don't necessarily know which one to aim for; and different options favor different people, making it a complex negotiation even if you can discuss the problem ahead of time.

There's a third important property which I've been assuming, but which doesn't follow so directly from the Folk Theorem: **the suboptimal equilibrium is "safe", in that you can unilaterally play that way to get some guaranteed utility.** The Pareto-optimal equilibria are not similarly safe; mistakenly playing one of them when other people don't can be worse than the "safe" guarantee from the poor equilibrium.

A game with all three properties is like Stag Hunt with multiple stags (where you all must hunt the same stag to win, but can hunt rabbit alone for a guaranteed mediocre payoff), or Schelling Pub where you can just stay home (you'd rather stay home than go out alone).

Lessons in Slaying Moloch

0. I didn't even address this in this essay, but it's worth mentioning: *not all conflicts are zero-sum*. In the introduction to the 1980 edition of *The Strategy of Conflict*, Thomas Schelling discusses the reception of the book. He recalls that a prominent political theorist "exclaimed how much this book had done for his thinking, and as he talked with enthusiasm I tried to guess which of my sophisticated ideas in which chapters had made so much difference to him. It turned out it wasn't any particular idea in any particular chapter. Until he read this book, he had simply not comprehended that an inherently non-zero-sum conflict could exist."

1. In situations such as iterated games, *there's no in-principle pull toward defection*. The Prisoner's Dilemma seems paradoxical when we first learn of it (at least, it seemed so to me) because we are not accustomed to such a harsh divide between individual incentives and the common good. But perhaps, as Sarah Constantin speculated in Don't Shoot the Messenger[5], modern game theory and economics have conditioned us to be used to this conflict due to their emphasis on single-shot interactions. As a result, Moloch comes to sound like an inevitable gravity, pulling everything downwards. This is not necessarily the case.

2. Instead, *most collective action problems are bargaining problems*. If a solution can be agreed upon, we can generally use

weak enforcement mechanisms (social norms) or strong enforcement (centralized governmental enforcement) to carry it out. But, agreeing about the solution may not be easy. The more parties involved, the more difficult the agreement becomes.

3. **Try to keep a path open toward better solutions.** Since wide adoption of a particular solution can be such an important problem, there's a tendency to treat alternative solutions as the enemy. This bars the way to further progress. (One could loosely characterize this as the difference between religious doctrine and democratic law; religious doctrine trades away the ability to improve in favor of the more powerful consensus-reaching technology of immutable universal law. But of course this oversimplifies things somewhat.) Keeping a path open for improvements is hard, partly because it can create exploitability. But it keeps us from getting stuck in a poor equilibrium.

Endnotes

(1) Comment by Raemon. Abram Demski. Most Prisoner's Dilemmas are Stag Hunts; Most Stag Hunts are Schelling Problems. 14th Sep 2020.

(2) Comment by Abram Demski. Raemon. The Schelling Choice is "Rabbit", not "Stag". 8th Jun 2019.

(3) Raemon. The Schelling Choice is "Rabbit", not "Stag". 8th Jun 2019.

(4) Zvi Mowshowitz. Immoral Mazes. 31st Dec 2019.

(5) Sarah Constantin. Don't Shoot the Messenger. 10th Apr 2017.

(6) https://egtheory.wordpress.com/

(7) Sarah Constantin. The Pavlov Strategy. 20th Dec 2018.

(8) Sarah Constantin. Contrite Strategies and The Need For Standards. 24th Dec 2018.

(9) Wikipedia. Folk theorem (game theory)

(10) https://www.lesswrong.com/tag/common-knowledge

(11) Eliezer Yudkowsky. Cooperating with agents with different ideas of fairness, while resisting exploitation. 16th Sep 2013.

Martin Sustrik

Swiss Political System: More Than You Ever Wanted to Know

T he Swiss political system may be best known for its extensive use of referenda. However, others may argue that its most striking feature is the ability to avoid political polarization. In this respect it may be unique among the western nations.

That being said, it is hard to learn much about how it works. First, a big part of the system is informal and thus only discoverable by observing it personally or by asking the locals. Second, it's strongly decentralized. Different rules apply in different cantons and municipalities which makes the topic confusing to study. Third, the Swiss aren't especially interested in promoting their own system abroad. A lot of the resources therefore exist only in local languages.

In this article I'll try to put together what I've learned by living in the country, speaking to local people, following local press and studying the resources.

Still, a disclaimer is due: I am not Swiss. I have lived here for only five years. Neither am I a political scientist or a sociologist. If you are Swiss, or simply know better than me, let me know about any inaccuracies in the article.

On the more technical side of things: There's a lot of material to cover, and the result may be rather overwhelming. It would be a small book rather than a long article. Therefore, this will be the first of multiple essays.

Semi-direct Democracy

When modern Switzerland was established in 1848, it was a pretty standard representative democracy, mostly based on the American model.

It's a federal state. Federal elections are held every four years. People are represented by political parties. There are two chambers of the parliament. Parliament elects members of the government, who then together run the country. The thriving ecosystem of various voluntary associations resembles the America that Alexis de Toqueville has written about.

However, Switzerland is special in that various elements of direct democracy were introduced over the course of history.

There are obligatory referenda: Any change in constitution, adjustment of taxes or joining of an international organization must be approved by the people and the cantons. There are legislative referenda: Any law enacted by the parliament may be challenged and rejected in a referendum. Finally, there are so called "popular initiatives" which can propose a referendum on any topic. If the initiative manages to collect a specified amount of signatures within a specified amount of time the referendum is organized and the initiative may eventually get enacted. All of these referenda exist not only on the federal, but also on the cantonal and the municipal level. All of them are binding and none of them need a quorum.

To understand the scope of the thing, consider that a 37-year-old from the city of Zurich who turned 18 in year 2000, has, in past 20 years, had the opportunity to take part in 548 referenda, 181 of them being on the federal, 176 on the cantonal and 191 on the municipal level. With the average turnout of 45% it means that they have voted in approximately 246 referenda.

Due to their large number, individual referenda are not organized separately. Instead, they are voted on in batches, typically four times a year.

To get a flavor of how it feels like, here's the batch from the city of Zurich in February 2020:

- Popular Initiative "Affordable Housing": A sensitive issue especially in big cities like Zurich or Geneva, where rents are some of the most expensive in the world. The initiative proposes to build at least 10% of affordable, non-profit or cooperative flats, as well as a pre-emptive right for cantons and municipalities to buy land. It also proposes that infrastructure upgrades should be done without reducing the number of available flats. The referendum is held at the federal level. 46.5% in favor. Rejected.

- Prohibition of discrimination on grounds of sexual orientation: Switzerland has previously prohibited discrimination on grounds of race, religion, age or political affiliation. This proposal adds sexual orientation to the list. Federal referendum. 63.52% in favor. Enacted.

- Law on passenger transport in taxis and limousines: a law that introduces the same rules for Uber and similar services and for the traditional taxi services. At the same time, it moves the enforcement of these rules from municipalities to the canton. The law was issued by the government of the canton of Zurich and challenged by a public initiative. (Not the least argument being that the law gives too much power to the canton at the expense of the municipalities.) Cantonal referendum. 52.84% in favor. Enacted.

- Rosengarten tunnel and tram project: A plan by the canton to put 1.1 billion francs into rebuilding the busiest street in Zurich and moving the traffic underground. The plan was challenged by a public initiative. Cantonal referendum. 36.32% in favor. Rejected.

- People's Initiative "Reduce the tax burden for lower and middle income people": An attempt to reduce income inequality. The proposal adjusts the cantonal taxes by raising the threshold for non-taxable income, as well as by increasing the tax burden in the highest income brackets. Cantonal referendum. 42.04% in favor. Rejected.

- Popular Initiative "Lower Taxes for Everyone": A proposal to reduce cantonal taxes for the highest income groups. The aim is to prevent the relocation of the wealthy people to tax havens such as the cantons of Zug or Schwyz. Cantonal referendum. 29.63% in favor. Rejected.

- Partial replacement of the tram depot in Hard district by new communal flats. The city proposes to take a loan of 203 million francs. Municipal referendum. 70.9% in favor. Enacted.

The canton publishes a handbook for each ballot, which explains, in quite a lot of detail, including graphs, maps and tables, what each referendum is about. Take the Rosengarten tunnel project. The guide devotes eight pages to explain the project, including topics such as the impact on the traffic situation in the canton, the impact on the environment, or a detailed explanation of the financing of the project. It states that both the cantonal government and parliament recommend voting in favor of the proposal. It is followed by the opinion of the minority in the cantonal parliament, arguing that the costs are too high, that the financial contribution from the federal government is uncertain, and that the project doesn't really address the existing problem. They recommend voting against. The next page contains the opinion of the parliament of the city of Zurich. They argue, in rather strong terms, against the project. Finally, there's the opinion of the referendum commission, which is, as one would expect, against the tunnel.

If even the election guide is not enough, you can have a look at the websites advocating for the yes and no vote, respectively. While the website against is relatively minimalist, the in favor side has a long list of supporters. In addition to almost all political parties, there's a long list of supportive associations: The Automobile Club, the Association for the Promotion of Public Transport, the Employers' Association, the Association of Construction Companies of Canton Schaffhausen, the Association of Small and Medium-sized Enterprises, the Property Owners' Association, Swiss Travel Club, Zurich Chamber of Commerce and the like. Many of these organizations have also published their own assessment of the project.

As can be seen, the voters aren't exposed to a simple, black and white choice. Instead, they are drawn into a complex network of different preferences: Your party is in favor, but the deputies of your municipality are against. You are a member of the automobile club and the club is in favor, but your neighbors are against. Voting necessarily means understanding that things are never clear-cut.

Mandatory Referenda

Any change to the constitution must be approved by the voters in a referendum. There's no way around it. If you want to change the constitution, you need the majority of voters and the majority of cantons to vote for it. Period. (To clarify: A canton is considered to be in favor if the majority of voters in the canton are in favor.)

While this may seem as a reasonable rule on its own, it is in fact an important piece that complements the overall system. The results of popular initiatives are, for example, written into the constitution, meaning that they can't be overturned, except by a different referendum. (On the other hand, it gives the Swiss Constitution a rather special character. It begins with the thundering: "In the name of Almighty God! We, the Swiss people and cantons, mindful of our responsibility to the Creation" etc., but then it ends with guidelines for the protection of swamps and rules for building holiday homes.)

Similarly, Switzerland has no constitutional court. The right to interpret the constitution is granted only to the people. They may do so by running a referendum that makes the wording of the constitution more clear.

In short, the system is crafted in such a way that there are no loopholes. No way to disrespect the popular opinion.

In addition to the changes to the constitution, referenda are also required in order to join international organizations. This way, Switzerland decided not to enter the European Economic Area in 1992, to join the Schengen area in 2005, not to join the UN in 1986 and, again, to join the UN in 2002. (And yes: Palace of Nations, the headquarters of the UN, is located in Geneva and was located there for a long time even before Switzerland became a member.)

Legislative Referenda

Legislative referenda get the least publicity but they may be the most important of all. Unlike constitutional referenda and public initiatives that tend to focus on big topics, the legislative referendum can challenge and reject any law, no matter how trivial, passed by the parliament.

This keeps the parliament and the government in check on a day-to-day basis. To quote Wikipedia:

The possibility for the citizens to challenge any law influences the whole political system. It encourages parties to form coalition governments, to minimize the risk that an important party tries to block the action of the government by systematically launching referendums. It gives legitimacy to political decisions. It forces the authorities to listen to all sectors of the population, to minimize the risk that they reject new laws in referendums. Before presenting a new bill to the parliament, the federal government usually makes a wide consultation to ensure that no significant group is frontally opposed to it, and willing to launch a referendum.

In short, legislative referenda are probably the single most important force driving Switzerland away from political polarization and towards rule by consensus.

Popular Initiatives

Popular initiative is a way to partially change the constitution in an arbitrary way.

As has already been said, if any proposal collects a hundred thousand signatures in a year and a half, it is voted upon in a referendum. The result of the vote is binding and there is no quorum. If just 1% of the population takes part and 0.51% votes in favor of the proposal, it will be enacted and implemented.

Also, there are no restrictions on the topic of the popular initiative. In some countries that have similar instrument in their constitution the topics are restricted. It may not be possible to hold referenda about basic human rights or maybe about taxes. Not so in Switzerland.

To understand what a popular initiative means, let's have a look at a little sample. What follows are all the popular initiatives on the federal level that were voted on in the 2015-2019 election period:

- "Stop urban spread." The Young Greens' initiative against suburbanization and for stricter zoning. 36.3% in favor. Rejected.

- "Swiss law instead of foreign law." Proposal for the Swiss constitution to take precedence over international treaties. Referendum initiated by the Swiss People's Party. 33.7% in favor. Rejected.

- "For cows with horns." An initiative initiated by farmer Armin Capaul. It proposed to subsidize the farmers who did not cut the cows' horns. 45.3% in favor. Rejected.

- "For food independence." A complex proposal to support farmers. It included a ban on genetically modified organisms. 31.6% in favor. Rejected.

- "Fair-food initiative." The Greens' attempt to introduce restrictions that would promote fair, environmentally friendly agriculture and prevent food waste. 38.7% in favor. Rejected.

- "For full-reserve banking." The initiative proposed that the Swiss National Bank should be the only source of money. Other banks would have to have cash reserves sufficient to pay out all the deposits. Initiative of the association "For the Modernization of Currency". 24.3% in favor. Rejected.

- "Against radio and television fees." Publicist Olivier Kessler's proposal to abolish fees for state-owned media. 28.4% in favor. Rejected.

- "For phasing out nuclear energy." An initiative launched by the Green Party. It proposed to decommission all the Swiss nuclear power plants by 2029. 45.8% in favor. Rejected.

- "For strong social insurance" An initiative of the largest Swiss trade union. It demanded to increase payments to social insurance by 10%. 40.6% in favor. Rejected.

- "For a green economy." The initiative called for the Swiss economy to function in a sustainable way. The government should set goals and report on how they are achieved at each session of the parliament. If the progress lags behind, additional measures should be taken. 36.6% in favor. Rejected.

- "For universal basic income." An initiative was initiated by several individuals. It proposed an unconditional regular income for all. The amount of income and the method of financing should be determined by law. 23.1% in favor. Rejected.

- The so-called "Dairy Cow" initiative. It suggested that the entirety of the fuel tax income should be spent on road maintenance. 29.2% in favor. Rejected.

- "Pro Public Service." The constitution should explicitly stipulate that state and semi-state organizations (post office, railways, telephone) are not run for financial gain. It should also limit the salaries of the employees in these organizations. 32.4% in favor. Rejected.

- "Stop food speculation!" Young Socialists' initiative. It proposed to ban certain financial instruments in the area of agricultural products. It ordered the Federal Government to combat such practices also at the international level. 40.1% in favor. Rejected.

- "For enforcing the expulsion of criminal aliens." Initiative of the Swiss People's Party. The party was dissatisfied with the government's implementation of the successful 2010 referendum on the expulsion of criminal aliens. 41.1% in favor. Rejected.

- "Against fines for marriage." The initiative of Christian Democrats, who did not like that in some cases unmarried couples paid fewer taxes than married couples. 49.2% in favor. Rejected.

Small cantonal or municipal popular initiatives are probably not that interesting for a reader from abroad, but still, let's mention a few of them. In recent years, the voters in the canton of Zurich have voted on: the definition of marriage as a union between a man and a woman; the expansion of the Stadelhofen railway station; the replacement of hunting associations by professional nature conservationists; the harmonization of school curricula in German-speaking cantons; having one instead of two compulsory foreign languages in schools; a law to support the film and gaming industry; economic organizations taking part in funding kindergartens; the abolition of the commission reviewing the claims of rejected asylum seekers; effective control of minimum wages. All of those initiatives were rejected.

It is also worth looking at the history of popular initiatives.

When modern Switzerland was founded in 1848 there was a clause in the constitution that the people could change the constitution. It was generally interpreted to mean that the constitution could only be replaced in its entirety. The instrument of the popular initiative was not established until 1891.

When we look at the list of all the popular initiatives, we notice that the instrument of popular initiative was little used at the beginning. The number of popular initiatives soars only in the seventies. The graph shows the number of all popular initiatives in grey and the number of successful ones in black.

The reason is that only by then did the instrument get working really smoothly.

In the beginning, for example, the custom of "putting the initiatives into the drawer" became established. The new initiatives were simply

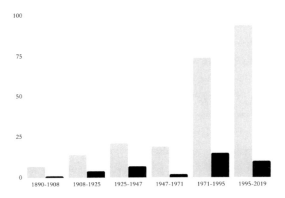

left in the vacuum, without a referendum, until they were forgotten, or until the initiative had lost all of its political relevance. One particular initiative was literally forgotten and canceled only after spending 43 years in a drawer.

After this system was heavily criticized in the press, the government eventually gave up on it.

The next trick was to make a government counter-proposal for a popular initiative and thus divide its supporters. If, say, 60% of the people were in favor of the initiative, the two proposals (the original proposal and the government's counter-proposal) divided them into two groups of 30% each, so that neither proposal passed.

This problem was solved in 1987 by the introduction of the so-called "double yes" which makes it possible to vote for both the initiative and the official counterproposal. An additional question was also introduced which asks which of the proposals one would favor if both proposals were successful.

Next, there is the problem of the validity of the referendum.

The Swiss constitution does not limit the subject of the popular initiative in any way. The only requirement it makes is that it has a coherent content. In practice, this means that the voter should never be forced to say yes or no to a question that mixes two unrelated matters. (Example: Do you want Putin to be able to run for a president for two more election periods and adjust the state pension in line with the inflation?)

So, for example, the popular initiative which called for a reduction in military spending and the use of the money for social purposes was canceled. The government's argument was that the financing of the army and the financing of social affairs are two independent issues that cannot be conflated in one referendum.

The argument sounds reasonable. But then one notices that some of the constitutional changes initiated by parliament are cheerfully mixing changes in various parts of the constitution. The system is unbalanced in this respect and the problem has not been solved yet.

Next, there is the problem of the consistency of the proposal with international treaties.

The first historical case had to do with a contract with Germany about the construction of a hydroelectric power plant in Rheinau on the border of the two states. According to the contract, the concession could not be canceled unilaterally. When the government, in 1954, allowed the popular initiative for the abolition of the power plant, it opened up the question of what happens if a referendum contradicts Switzerland's international commitments.

Back in the day, Switzerland avoided embarrassment because the initiative against the Rheinau power plant was not successful. In recent years, however, there have been a couple of successful initiatives that contradicted international treaties.

One of them was the initiative for the automatic expulsion of criminal aliens in 2010. As the result of the referendum was never properly put into practice, in 2018 the original author of the initiative (Swiss People's Party) came up with a different initiative proposing that the Swiss constitution - and therefore the results of the popular initiatives - should always take precedence to international law, with the exception of those international treaties that were approved in a referendum.

Should such a referendum pass, Switzerland could at any time revoke its existing international obligations and would be considered an unreliable partner abroad. Which, of course, could be a serious problem for Switzerland's export-oriented economy.

However, the referendum did not pass and so the problem is still unresolved. We can only guess how it will turn out. Maybe, one day, all international treaties will be voted on to gain unquestionable legitimacy. However, even this will not solve the problem of already existing international treaties and retroactive changes through popular initiatives.

To explore another serious and hard-to-fix flaw in the Swiss political system, let's have a look at the initiative "Against Mass Immigration".

First, some background.

Immigration is a serious issue in Switzerland. In that it differs from certain countries, including my native Slovakia, where immigration is negligible, but it is nevertheless used as a bogeyman to score political points. In Switzerland, a quarter of the country's population does not have Swiss citizenship. In city cantons such as Zurich or Geneva, the proportion of foreigners is even higher. There are even a lot of third generation immigrants who still don't hold a Swiss passport.

The problem began after the second world war, when Switzerland, spared by the war, became an attractive country to immigrate to. People started moving in and that caused political tensions, as witnessed by no less than seven referenda against immigration between the years of 1968 and 2000. As Max Frisch once pointedly noted: "We asked for workers. We got people instead."

The number of non-citizens is nowadays so high that it's not only the xenophobes who lose their sleep. Traditional conservatives are worried as well: Is it possible to preserve the existing communal and political culture with that many foreigners? And so are liberals: Can a country where a quarter of the population doesn't have the right to vote still be called a democracy?

After all the anti-immigration referenda failed during the second half of the 20th century (support varied from 29.5% to 46.3%), the initiative "Against Mass Immigration" finally succeeds in 2014 with 50.33% of the vote in favor. It asks for introducing quotas for foreigners, such that they "align with Switzerland's economic interests and favor Swiss citizens."

The government announces that it will act quickly and pass the necessary legislation before the end of the year. One week after the referendum, the Swiss Minister of Justice calls the Croatian Minister of Foreign Affairs and informs her that Switzerland won't sign the draft agreement, which gives Croatia (then a new EU member state) free access to the Swiss labor market.

The European Commission responds that one can't cherry-pick from the freedoms enshrined in the treaty and that restricting freedom of movement will jeopardize Swiss access to the single European market. Brussels promptly suspends talks on cooperation in the sphere of education (Erasmus+ project with the budget of €14.7 billion for the next six years) and science (Horizon 2020, €80 billion budget for the same period). It also suspends talks on integrating the Swiss electricity market into the European market.

Universities report estimated losses on research grants in the order of hundreds of millions of euros. The government itself estimates that exclusion from Horizon 2020 will jeopardize 8,000 jobs. Higher electricity prices are expected. The student union is protesting because students suddenly do not know if they will be able to start the planned student exchanges. Credit Suisse is lowering its estimate of Swiss economic growth (from 1.9% to 1.6%) and expects that about 80,000 fewer jobs will be created.

The government finds itself between a rock and a hard place. After three years, just a few months before the deadline for implementing the referendum expires, it abandons the idea of immigration quotas and introduces a few half-hearted bureaucratic obstacles to employing EU citizens.

The country suddenly finds itself in an uncomfortable situation where the law is, strictly speaking, in conflict with the constitution. (Recall that the results of referenda are written into the constitution.) At the same time, Switzerland does not have a constitutional court, which would reject the offending laws. Only the people are supposed to interpret the constitution through a referendum.

To appreciate how dangerous that is, consider that the Swiss system of direct democracy is based on the people modifying the constitution and the government subsequently implementing those changes in law. If the government starts to disregard the constitution, the system collapses. People may vote for whatever they want and it would have no effect. They can, in theory, challenge unconstitutional laws in legislative referenda, but interpreting hundreds of pages of legalese is probably too much to ask from an ordinary citizen. At the same time, there's no legal instrument to either challenge a standing law after it's in place for 100 days or to introduce a new law by means of a referendum.

To be fair, a new form of initiative, the so called "general popular initiative", was introduced by the government in 2003 to allow for changing federal law. The instrument was approved in a referendum (70.3% in favor) but later it turned out that a lot of voters had no idea what it was about. In fact, it turned out that even the government didn't have a good idea. When they tried to implement it they found out that there were so many pitfalls and complications that it wasn't feasible. In 2008 they proposed that the new instrument be removed from the constitution and the people approved the removal in a referendum (67.9% in favor).

In any case, the story continues with the People's party, the initiator of the anti-immigration referendum shouting treason, but then announcing that they will not challenge the decision in another referendum. Instead, they opt to challenge the outcome indirectly, with an initiative asking for Swiss law - and thus the outcome of the anti-mass immigration initiative - to take precedence over international treaties, and thus over the Treaty on Free Movement with the EU. The initiative is rejected in a referendum.

In 2018, signature collection begins for a new referendum. The proposal instructs the government to negotiate the removal of free movement clauses from the treaties with the European Union and, if that does not happen, establishes automatic termination of said treaties. The referendum was scheduled for May 2020, but postponed due to the coronavirus epidemic. That being said, at the time of writing the surveys show that the referendum will most likely fail and the problem of discrepancy between the constitution and the law will persist.

To conclude, it is worth noting how the discussion is becoming more and more nuanced over the years. In the 19th century, it was disputed whether a partial change in the constitution through a popular initiative was permissible at all. Then we see the government openly sabotaging the legal instrument. Today, 130 years after it was introduced, the Swiss are finally dealing with the actual messy problems that the usage of popular initiatives entails.

Dangerous Referenda

A common argument against referenda is that they are dangerous. Let's recall how Lukashenko entrenched himself in power: The referendum in 1995 gave him the power to dissolve the parliament. In 1996, again in a referendum, Belarusians decided that the presidential decrees would have force of law. Finally, the referendum in 2004 extended the presidential term indefinitely.

Or, for that matter, recall the Brexit referendum and the political chaos it plunged the UK into.

Given this danger and the fact - quite noticeable in the previous sample - that 90% of the popular initiatives tend to be rejected, one has to ask whether Switzerland gains any benefits from using the instrument at all.

But contemplating it, one may wonder whether the fact that out of all 210 popular initiatives that were voted on since 1891 only 22 were successful is besides the point. Perhaps it doesn't matter how many initiatives are being rejected. Perhaps the only thing that matters is that there's a safeguard when a conflict of interest between the people and their elected representatives arises. In such a situation a popular initiative may adjust the political system in such a way as to align the interests of the representatives with the interests of the people anew.

But as we look at the successful popular initiatives, we see almost no cases of such initiatives. At least at first glance, it is not clear why the topic of swamp protection or the topic of the construction of holiday homes should lead to a conflict of this kind.

However, two historical initiatives are an exception to the rule.

Back in 1917 Switzerland used to use a majority system in the parliamentary elections. This led to a situation where the Liberal Democrats got only 40.8% of the vote, but 54.5% of the seats in parliament. The absolute majority allowed them to pass the laws, regardless of the will of the 59.2% who voted for other parties.

Needless to say, the Liberal Democrats torpedoed every attempt to replace the majority voting system by a proportional one. If the instrument of popular initiatives was not available, it would be a dead end. The voters would have to wait until Liberal Democrats lose some of their voter support. But even then, thanks to the majority system, an absolute majority in parliament could be won by another party, who would again find it difficult to abolish the system that brought it to power.

General dissatisfaction with the state of affairs led to the launch of the popular initiative "For a proportional system of elections to the National Council" in 1918 which succeeded with 66.8% votes in favor.

In 1919, elections were finally held using the new, proportional system and Liberal Democrats lost the absolute majority.

The second exception happened in the period after World War II. During the war, a state of emergency was declared, in which a large number of otherwise decentralized powers were transferred to the federal government. After the war, the government refused to relinquish those powers. In 1949, however, the popular initiative "For a Return to Direct Democracy" (50.7% in favor) returned matters to the pre-war state.

But however important those two exceptions may be, do they justify the existence of popular initiatives? To justify a powerful and dangerous instrument like that, one would expect to gain at least some day-to-day advantage rather than something that happens twice in a century.

Well, it turns out that referenda, in fact, serve an important day-to-day purpose: They act as a sword hanging over the parliament and the government.

Consider the legislative referendum. It can be used to block any law passed by parliament. The consequence, which, while obvious, does not occur immediately, is that the parliament simply does not pass laws that are apparently going to be challenged and rejected in a referendum.

Often, even a threat of referendum is enough to cause a change in the law or even let it be dropped altogether.

What's more, both the government and the parliament are very well aware of the possibility of a referendum and so they proactively make sure that no significant group of the population has a reason to block the new law.

Additionally, a zero quorum for a referendum means that even small minorities must be taken into account: If the law discriminates against, say, the hearing impaired, the rest of the nation may well ignore the referendum, but the deaf and deaf-mute will still be able to force its abolition.

The popular initiatives complement the system: Legislative referenda can be used only to reject new laws. Popular initiatives can be used to challenge old and dysfunctional ones.

And now it's becoming clear why almost all popular initiatives are rejected. If the initiative had a obvious chance of being approved, the parliament would introduce the necessary legislation on its own. From this point of view the small number of successful initiatives is not a sign of a system malfunction, but rather a proof that the system is functioning the way it is expected to.

In some cases it happens that the initiative has a chance to pass, but the government or parliament considers it harmful or disadvantageous. In these cases, they can come up with a so-called counter-proposal. The counter-proposal is typically a compromise. If the initiative asks for

100, the counter-proposal offers 50. Voters can then choose between rejecting the initiative altogether, accepting it, or accepting the counter-proposal.

In 2014, for example, the Evangelical Party of canton Zurich initiates a popular initiative for reducing the size of classes in schools. The initiative proposes a cap of 20 students per class. The cantonal parliament offers a counter-proposal in which it promises to create 100 new teaching jobs and distribute those teachers preferentially into municipalities that suffer the most from the problems with large class sizes. In the end, voters opted for the government counter-proposal.

The efficiency of the system of counter-proposals is witnessed not only by them being accepted on quite a regular basis, but also by the fact that 73 federal popular initiatives were, in the course of history, withdrawn by their initiators in favor of the government counter-proposals.

There are yet more functions of popular initiatives.

To understand the next one, consider the process that each initiative goes through: The Federal Council will first check the referendum and translate it into all official languages. Then, the signatures are collected. The limit for collecting a sufficient number of signatures is one year and a half. The signature sheets are then handed over to the Federal Council. The government has a year and a half to discuss the proposal. If it decides to file a counter-proposal, this period is extended by another year and a half. Consultations with experts and all the stakeholders are held within this time. The government prepares a detailed report and passes it to the parliament. Parliament has another year and a half to discuss it. In the case of a counter-proposal, the period can be prolonged to three and a half years. Finally, the government sets a date for the referendum, which must happen within the next ten months.

The whole initiative, from the draft proposal to the vote, can therefore take up to nine years. In practice, this period usually ranges from two to six years.

The process seems highly inefficient at a first glance, but when one listens to what Swiss political scientists have to say on the matter, it becomes clear that this sluggishness is not a bug, but rather a feature. Some even distinguish between a real referendum (in Switzerland) and a plebiscite (everywhere else). One important difference is that the long duration of the process, which spans across election periods, prevents the referendum from being used for tactical purposes. Another difference is that it provides ample time for in-depth public debate.

And there's a lot of debate. It is not just the consultations organized by the government and parliament. The referenda are discussed in the media, both in serious newspapers and in tabloids, which are handed out for free at tram stops. They are discussed among colleagues at work during lunch. They are discussed within the family during dinner. At night they are discussed in pubs and bars. Associations, companies, political parties, government, parliament, all kinds of organizations and individuals all recommend voting either in favor or against. Public discussions are organized. Every simpleton feels obligated to express himself on the subject.

When election day comes, one may get an election handbook that presents both sides of the argument, but at that moment, one's head is already filled with various arguments, both in favor and against. One has become, at least to some extent, an expert on the subject. (And if you think about it, the 548 referenda in Zurich in the past 20 years mean that the educational aspect of the system may be surprisingly large.)

To put the above in different words, a popular initiative can also be understood as a call for a public debate on a certain topic. The fact that it is followed by a binding vote ensures that people actually do care about the debate. True, the vast majority of popular initiatives are rejected, but at that point there has been a public discourse and people are at least aware of the matter. With referenda on matters such as universal basic income or full reserve banking, one would expect widening of the Overton window[1]. However, I wasn't able to find a study comparing the size of the window in Switzerland and elsewhere.

One can also think of the public debate as a safety measure. Particular initiatives may be dangerous, if approved, but when people go to ballots they are already well aware of the danger.

Another safety measure is that Swiss referenda are, in their essence, not polarizing. In referendum you are never asked to decide between two extremes, between, say, pro-life and pro-choice, but rather between the initiative proposal and the status quo. Voting against is always a safe and neutral option. It doesn't necessarily mean that you are not sympathetic to the spirit of the initiative. You may just think it's going too far, or maybe you like some aspects of it but don't like others.

Consider the 2013 vote on the law granting special powers to the government in the case of an epidemic. Some people were against the proposal because they thought it makes the federal government too powerful. At the same time they've kept quiet about it because they haven't wanted to be seen as part of the anti-vaxxer crowd which was dominating the debate. Luckily, voting against was a neutral choice they could take advantage of. It didn't mean that vaccination programmes would be relaxed. It just meant that the status quo would be preserved.

Referenda as Tools: The Jurassic Question

The history of the Jurassic question begins after the Napoleonic Wars, in 1815, when the Jura region, traditionally part of the Principality-Bishopric of Basel, was annexed to the canton of Bern.

Jura, however, unlike Bern, is French-speaking and to make the situation worse, while the southern part of Jura is predominantly Protestant, same as Bern, the northern part of it is Catholic.

So, starting in 1826, several separatist movements emerge in Jura, fueled mainly by religious frictions, the question of the separation of church and state, and later, to some extent, nationalism based on the language.

Modern Jurassic separatism dates back to 1947, when the Bern cantonal parliament refused to grant the position of construction minister to Jurassic politician Georges Moeckli on the grounds that he doesn't speak Bernese dialect well enough. That has opened old wounds.

The following events are chaotic. The emergence of different opposition movements, mutual insults, demonstrations, public burning of a civil defense handbook, demolition of a statue of an unknown soldier, occupation of Swiss embassies abroad, bombs, paving stones and, unfortunately, several casualties.

In short, the whole range of events that accompany separatist movements around the world.

However, unlike in Northern Ireland, where the violence spiralled out of control at approximately the same time, Switzerland succeeded - not least through the extensive use of the instruments of direct democracy - in keeping the situation under control and eventually, if at the typically sluggish Swiss pace, resolving it.

We can't go into details here, but let's at least look at a short timeline:

- 1968: Establishment of two commissions (one bilateral and one impartial) to propose a plan to address the Jurassic question.

- March 1970: The plan is approved in a referendum. The following referendums are proceeding according to the approved plan.

- June 1974: Referendum on whether to create a new canton of Jura. Approved.

- March 1975: Districts that voted against the new canton in a previous referendum to decide their fate. The southern, Protestant part of the Jura decides to remain in the canton of Bern.

- Autumn 1975: Municipalities at the border between the two cantons decide in referenda whether to join Bern or Jura.

- September 1978: In a federal referendum, the Swiss constitution is amended to list the new canton (82.3% of the vote in favor).

Note the architectural beauty of the process. How the referendum is cleverly used to relieve the tension. Step by step, in cold blood, room for manoeuvre is taken from those who benefit from inciting conflict.

Firstly, the referendum on the process of resolving the issue was separated from the referendum on the issue itself. The fact that the process was approved in advance in a referendum gave legitimacy to the following referendums on specific issues and, the other way round, deprived the subsequent attempts to challenge the results of legitimacy.

Secondly, the fact that the process proposed by the preparatory commission had to be subsequently approved in a referendum created pressure in the commission to find a compromise solution. If they leaned too far to one side, there was a risk that the process would be rejected in the referendum and that the entire work of the commission would end up in the trash, along with the political careers of everyone involved.

Thirdly, note how, in the sequence of referendums, it was only those territorial units that voted against the winning solution that got an additional vote. That prevented unending oscillation between Bern and Jura. The number of disputed areas kept constantly decreasing with each subsequent step of the process.

Finally, the ongoing process siphoned the moderates, who would otherwise have no option but to join radicals, towards peaceful campaigning for the oncoming referenda.

The events do not end with the creation of the new canton in 1979 though.

In the referenda above, the municipality of Laufen decided to remain in the canton of Bern, creating a Bern enclave between the cantons of Jura, Solothurn and Basel-Country. The events continued as follows:

- November 1977: popular initiative "Do you want to start the process of connecting Laufen to the neighboring canton?" succeeds with 65% of the votes in favor.

- January 1980: Referendum precludes Laufen joining the canton of Basel-City.

- March 1980: In yet another referendum, Laufen decides to start negotiations with the canton of Basel-Country (64.65% in favor).

- September 1983: Unsuccessful referendum on joining the canton of Basel-Country. 56.68% vote against. Laufen remains in the canton of Bern. (A parallel referendum in the canton of Basel-Country approves the adoption of Laufen by a majority of 73% of the votes.)

- 1985: A scandal with discovery of the secret fund to finance Bernese loyalists in Laufen. The Bern Parliament rejects the complaint of the citizens of Lausanne. They bring the case before the Federal Court. The court orders a new referendum.

- November 1989: Laufen decides to join the canton of Basel-Country (51.72% in favor).

- September 1991: The canton of Basel-Country votes to accept Laufen. The decision is less warm than in 1983, but the referendum still passes (59.3% in favor).

- September 1993: Federal referendum approves the annexation of Laufen to the canton of Basel-Country (75.2% in favor).

But the question of the so-called Bernese Jura (Protestant parts of Jura that have not joined the new canton) is still not resolved to the general satisfaction. Separatists haven't yet given up.

In February 2012 the governments of the cantons of Bern and Jura agree to deliver a solution to the problem. In November 2013, two referenda are held, one in Jura, the other in Bernese Jura. The referenda pose the question of whether to begin the process of creating a new canton that would include both areas. Should the referendum pass, a commission would be set up to propose a detailed process, which would then be voted upon in a referendum. The preliminary idea was that every municipality in the Bernese Jura would vote on whether to stay in the canton of Bern or join the canton of Jura.

Although the referendum succeeds in the canton of Jura (64.2% in favor), it fails in Berenese Jura (28.15% in favor). Thus, the question of the Great Jura is definitely off the table. Any further inciting of the Jurassic question loses political legitimacy.

The last painful spot is the town of Moutier, the only district in Bernese Jura which voted for the creation of the Great Jura (55% in favor).

Shortly after the previous referendum, the city of Moutier decides to hold a municipal referendum on joining the canton of Jura.

- January 2016: The canton of Bern approves the referendum.

- June 2017: The referendum accepts the joining of the canton of Jura (51.72% of the vote in favor).

- November 2018: The prefecture of Bernese Jura complains about the irregularities in the referendum and declares the result invalid.

- October 2019: After the Bernese court confirmed the abolition of the referendum, the city council decides not to pursue the matter in front of the federal court, but rather to hold a new referendum in 2020.

And so, if everything goes well, the Jurassic question will be definitively resolved soon, after more than two centuries of conflict.

Endnotes

(1) Wikipedia. Overton Window.

Jason Crawford

Why haven't we celebrated any major achievements lately

This is a linkpost for https://rootsofprogress.org/celebrations-of-progress

In reading stories of progress, one thing that has struck me was the wild, enthusiastic celebrations that accompanied some of them in the past. Read some of these stories. Somehow it's hard for me to imagine similar jubilation happening today:

The US transcontinental railroad, 1869

The transcontinental railroad was the first to link the US east and west. Prior to the railroad, to travel from coast to coast could take six months, whether by land or sea, and the journey was hard and perilous. California was like a foreign colony, separated from the life and industry of the East. The railroad changed that completely, taking a six-month journey down to a matter of *days*.

Here's how the western cities reacted, from Stephen Ambrose's book *Nothing Like It in the World*[1]:

> At 5 A.M. on Saturday, a Central Pacific train pulled into Sacramento carrying celebrants from Nevada, including firemen and a brass band. They got the festivities going by starting their parade. A brass cannon, the very one that had saluted the first shovelful of earth Leland Stanford had turned over for the beginning of the CP's construction six years earlier, boomed once again.

> The parade was mammoth. At its height, about 11 A.M. in Sacramento, the time the organizers had been told the joining of the rails would take place, twenty-three of the CP's locomotives, led by its first, the Governor Stanford, let loose a shriek of whistles that lasted for fifteen minutes.

> In San Francisco, the parade was the biggest held to date. At 11 A.M., a fifteen-inch Parrott rifled cannon at Fort Point, guarding the south shore of the Golden Gate, fired a salute. One hundred guns followed.

Then fire bells, church bells, clock towers, machine shops, streamers, foundries, the U.S. Mint let go at full blast. The din lasted for an hour.

In both cities, the celebration went on through Saturday, Sunday, and Monday.

The Brooklyn Bridge, 1883

The Brooklyn Bridge did not connect a distance nearly as great as the transcontinental railroad, but it too was met with grand celebrations. An excerpt from David McCullough's *The Great Bridge*[2]:

> When the Erie Canal was opened in the autumn of 1825, there were four former Presidents of the United States present in New York City for the occasion—John Adams, Thomas Jefferson, James Madison, and James Monroe—as well as John Quincy Adams, then occupying the White House, and General Andrew Jackson, who would take his place. When the Brooklyn Bridge was opened on May 24, 1883, the main attraction was Chester A. Arthur. ...
>
> Seth Low made the official greeting for the City of Brooklyn, the Marines presented arms, a signal flag was dropped nearby and instantly there was a crash of a gun from the Tennessee. Then the whole fleet commenced firing. Steam whistles on every tug, steamboat, ferry, every factory along the river, began to scream. More cannon boomed. Bells rang, people were cheering wildly on every side. The band played

"Hail to the Chief" maybe six or seven more times, and as the New York Sun reported, "the climax of fourteen years' suspense seemed to have been reached, since the President of the United States of America had walked dry shod to Brooklyn from New York."

Not only did they celebrate, they analyzed and philosophized:

What was it all about? What was everyone celebrating? The speakers of the day had a number of ideas. The bridge was a "wonder of Science," an "astounding exhibition of the power of man to change the face of nature." It was a monument to "enterprise, skill, faith, endurance." It was also a monument to "public spirit," "the moral qualities of the human soul," and a great, everlasting symbol of "Peace." The words used most often were "Science," "Commerce," and "Courage," and some of the ideas expressed had the familiar ring of a Fourth of July oration. …

… every speaker that afternoon seemed to be saying that the opening of the bridge was a national event, that it was a triumph of human effort, and that it somehow marked a turning point. It was the beginning of something new, and although none of them appeared very sure what was going to be, they were confident it would be an improvement over the past and present.

The celebrations culminated with an enormous fireworks show:

In all, fourteen tons of fireworks—more than ten thousand pieces—were set off from the bridge. It lasted a solid hour. There was not a moment's letup. One meteoric burst followed another. ...

... finally, at nine, as the display on the bridge ended with one incredible barrage—five hundred rockets fired all at once—every whistle and horn on the river joined in. The rockets "broke into millions of stars and a shower of golden rain which descended upon the bridge and the river." Bells were rung, gongs were beaten, men and women yelled themselves hoarse, musicians blew themselves red in the face.

Comparing this to another accomplishment we'll return to below, McCullough writes:

In another time and in what would seem another world, on a day when two young men were walking on the moon, a very old woman on Long Island would tell reporters that the public excitement over the feat was not so much compared to what she had seen "on the day they opened the Brooklyn Bridge."

Electric lighting, 1879

The electric light bulb was perhaps not met with parades or fireworks, but it did attract visitors from far and wide just to see the marvel. From Robert Gordon's *The Rise and Fall of American Growth*:

Few, if any inventions, have been more
enthusiastically welcomed than electric light.
Throughout the winter of 1879–1880, thousands
traveled to Menlo Park to see the "light of the
future," including farmers whose houses would
never be electrified in their lifetimes. Travelers on the
nearby Pennsylvania Railroad could see the brilliant
lights glowing in the Edison offices. The news was
announced to the world on December 21, 1879, with
a full-page story in the New York Herald, opened by
this dramatic and long-winded headline: EDISON'S
LIGHT—THE GREAT INVENTOR'S TRIUMPH
IN ELECTRIC ILLUMINATION—A SCRAP OF
PAPER—IT MAKES A LIGHT, WITHOUT GAS
OR FLAME, CHEAPER THAN OIL—SUCCESS
IN A COTTON THREAD. On New Year's Eve of
1879, 3,000 people converged by train, carriage, and
farm wagon on the Edison laboratory to witness the
brilliant display, a planned laboratory open house of
dazzling modernity to launch the new decade.

The polio vaccine, 1955

Rails, bridges and lights were celebrated in part because they greatly
relieved the burdens of distance and darkness. Another burden was
lifted in 1955 when the polio vaccine was announced.

Polio *terrified* the nation, much more so than diseases such as
tuberculosis that were actually much bigger killers, for a few reasons.
It struck in unpredictable, dramatic epidemics. The epidemics were
relatively new starting in the late 1800s; it was not a disease that had

been widespread throughout history, such as smallpox$_3$. It left many victims paralyzed rather than killing them, so its results were visible in the form of crutches, braces, and wheelchairs. It targeted children, striking fear into the hearts of parents. And it could not be fought with the new weapons of cleanliness and sanitation, which were successful against so many other diseases. This added guilt to the fear, as parents of polio victims obsessed over what they had done wrong in failing to protect their children.

So it's understandable that the entire nation was eager to hear the news of a vaccine, and went wild when it was achieved. From *Breakthrough: The Saga of Jonas Salk*, by Richard Carter:

> On April 12, 1955, the world learned that a vaccine developed by Jonas Edward Salk, M.D., could be relied upon to prevent paralytic poliomyelitis. This news consummated the most extraordinary undertaking in the history of science, a huge research project led by a Wall Street lawyer and financed by the American people through hundreds of millions of small donations. More than a scientific achievement, the vaccine was a folk victory, an occasion for pride and jubilation. A contagion of love swept the world. People observed moments of silence, rang bells, honked horns, blew factory whistles, fired salutes, kept their traffic lights red in brief periods of tribute, took the rest of the day off, closed their schools or convoked fervid assemblies therein, drank toasts, hugged children, attended church, smiled at strangers, forgave enemies....
>
> The ardent people named schools, streets, hospitals, and newborn infants after him. They sent him checks,

cash, money orders, stamps, scrolls, certificates, pressed flowers, snapshots, candy, baked goods, religious medals, rabbits' feet and other talismans, and uncounted thousands of letters and telegrams, both individual and round-robin, describing their heartfelt gratitude and admiration. They offered him free automobiles, agricultural equipment, clothing, vacations, lucrative jobs in government and industry, and several hundred opportunities to get rich quick. Their legislatures and parliaments passed resolutions, and their heads of state issued proclamations. Their universities tendered honorary degrees. He was nominated for the Nobel prize, which he did not get, and a Congressional medal, which he got, and membership in the National Academy of Sciences, which turned him down. He was mentioned for several dozen lesser awards of national or local or purely promotional character, most of which he turned down.

Not all of this happened on April 12, 1955, but much of it did. Salk awakened that morning as a moderately prominent research professor on the faculty of the University of Pittsburgh School of Medicine. He ended the day as the most beloved medical scientist on earth.

David Oshinsky adds more details in *Polio: An American Story*[4]:

There had been celebrations like this for athletes, soldiers, politicians, aviators—but never for a scientist. Gifts and honors poured in from a grateful nation. Philadelphia awarded Salk its Poor Richard

Medal for distinguished service to humanity. Mutual of Omaha gave him its Criss Award, along with a $10,000 check, for his contribution to public health. The University of Pittsburgh was swamped with thank-you notes and "donations" addressed to Dr. Salk. His lab was "knee-deep in mail," a staffer recalled. "Paper money [went] into one bin, checks into another, and metal coins into a third." (How much was collected, and who kept what, was never fully divulged.) Elementary schools sent giant posters—WE LOVE YOU DR. SALK—signed by the entire student body. Winnipeg, Canada, site of a major polio epidemic in 1953, sent a 208-foot telegram of congratulation adorned with each survivor's name. A town in the Texas panhandle bought him two heartfelt, if comically inappropriate, gifts: a plow and a fully equipped Oldsmobile 98. (Salk gave the plow to an orphanage and had the car sold so the town could buy more polio vaccine.) A new Cadillac arrived and was donated to charity. Colleges begged him to accept their honorary degrees. Newsweek lauded "A Quiet Young Man's Magnificent Victory," insisting that Salk's name was now "as secure a word in the medical dictionary as Jenner, Pasteur, Schick, and Lister."

Hollywood wasn't far behind. Three major studios—Warner Brothers, Columbia, and Twentieth Century-Fox—fought for the exclusive rights to Salk's life story. Rumors flew that Marlon Brando was angling for the lead—an odd choice, most agreed, but a sure sign of box office pizzazz. Salk wisely told them no. "I believe that such pictures are most appropriately made after the scientist is dead," he remarked, "and I'm willing to await my chances of such attention at that time."

Politicians embraced him. One senator introduced a bill to give the forty-year-old Salk a $10,000 annual stipend for life. Another proposed the minting of a Salk dime, just like FDR's. (Both ideas went nowhere.) Governor George Leader of Pennsylvania gave him the state's highest honor—the Bronze Medal for Meritorious Service—before a cheering joint session of the legislature (which soon created an endowed chair for Salk at the University of Pittsburgh Medical School with a princely stipend of $25,000 a year). On an even grander scale, the U.S. House and Senate began the bipartisan process of commissioning a Congressional Gold Medal, the nation's highest civilian award. Salk would become only the second medical researcher to receive one, joining Walter Reed of yellow fever fame. The two men were in good company. Previous honorees included Thomas Edison, Charles Lindbergh, General George C. Marshall, and Irving Berlin.

Hundreds wrote President Eisenhower to request a special White House ceremony for Salk. ... On April 22 Jonas and Donna Salk, their three young boys, and Basil O'Connor arrived at the White House to meet the president. ... The Rose Garden ceremony that day would not soon be forgotten. Few had ever seen Dwight Eisenhower struggle with his feelings in such a public way. "No bands played and no flags waved," wrote a reporter who had followed Ike for years. "But nothing could have been more impressive than this grandfather standing there and telling Dr. Salk in a voice trembling with emotion, 'I have no words to thank you. I am very, very happy.'"

… The banner headline in the Pittsburgh Press on April 12, 1955 had set the tone—POLIO IS CONQUERED. The stories that day spoke of mothers weeping, doctors cheering, politicians toasting God and Jonas Salk.

Steven Pinker, in *Enlightenment Now*[5], after quoting some of the passage from Richard Carter above, adds: "The city of New York offered to honor Salk with a ticker-tape parade, which he politely declined." Speaking of which—

Historic flights, 1920s and '30s

I looked up the history of ticker-tape parades in New York City. Wikipedia has a list[6]. These seem to have been most common from about 1926 to 1965, with multiple parades a year in that period (except when the US was fighting WW2, when there were none), compared with less than one a year on average in the years before or since.

What was celebrated? Mostly politicians, military heroes, visiting foreign leaders, and occasionally sports champions. (There was one parade for a musician, Van Cliburn, after he won the Moscow International Tchaikovsky Competition.)

However, the 1920s and '30s saw over a dozen parades celebrating aviation achievements, including Charles Lindburgh and Amelia Earhart:

- 1926, June 23—Commander Richard Byrd and Floyd Bennett, flight over the North Pole.

- 1927, June 13—Charles Lindbergh, following solo transatlantic flight.

- 1927, July 18—"Double" parade for Commander Richard Byrd and the crew of the America; and for Clarence Chamberlin and Charles A. Levine following separate transatlantic flights.

- 1927, November 11—Ruth Elder and George W. Haldeman following flight from New York City to the Azores.

- 1928, April 25—Hermann Köhl, Major James Fitzmaurice, and Baron von Hünefeld following first westward transatlantic flight.

- 1928, July 6—Amelia Earhart, Wilmer Stultz, and Louis E. Gordon.

- 1930, September 4—Captain Dieudonne Coste and Maurice Bellonte following flight from Paris to New York City.

- 1931, July 2—Wiley Post and Harold Gatty following round-the-world flight.

- 1932, June 20—Amelia Earhart Putnam following transatlantic flight.

- 1933, July 21—Air Marshal Italo Balbo and crew for flight from Rome to Chicago in 25 Italian seaplanes.

- 1933, July 26—Wiley Post following eight-day round-the-world flight.

- 1933, August 1—Captain James A. Mollison and his wife following westward transatlantic flight, from Wales to Connecticut.

- 1938, July 15—Howard Hughes, following three-day flight around the world.

- 1938, August 5—Douglas "Wrong Way" Corrigan following flight from New York City to Ireland (he was scheduled to fly to California).

Astronauts, 1962–71

During the early space program, there were also several NYC ticker-tape parades for astronauts—not just the Apollo 11 heroes, who went on a world tour after the Moon landing, but missions before and after as well:

- 1962, March 1—John Glenn, following the Mercury-Atlas 6 mission.

- 1962, June 5—Scott Carpenter, following the Mercury 7 mission.

- 1963, May 22—Gordon Cooper, following the Mercury 9 mission.

- 1965, March 29—Virgil "Gus" Grissom and John Young, following the Gemini 3 mission.

- 1969, January 10—Frank Borman, James A. Lovell, and William A. Anders, following the Apollo 8 mission to the Moon.

- 1969, August 13—Neil Armstrong, Buzz Aldrin, and Michael Collins, following Apollo 11 mission to the Moon.

- 1971, March 8 - Alan Shepard, Edgar Mitchell, and Stuart Roosa, following Apollo 14 mission to the Moon.

- 1971, August 24 - David Scott, James Irwin, and Alfred Worden, following Apollo 15 mission to the Moon.

And much later:

1998, November 16—John Glenn and astronauts of Space Shuttle Discovery mission STS-95.

Apollo 11 parade. Wikimedia / NASA[7].

Recent celebrations?

I'm having a hard time coming up with any major celebrations of scientific, technological, or industrial achievements since the Apollo Program.

When I alluded to this on Twitter[8], some people suggested the long lines of consumers waiting to buy iPhones. I don't count that in the same category: it shows a desire for a product. I'm looking for outright celebration.

It's not that no one cares about progress anymore. Plenty of people still get excited by science news, new inventions, and breakthrough achievements—especially in space, which has a strong "coolness" factor. Noah Smith polled his followers[9], and ~75% of respondents said they "celebrated or got very excited about" the Mars Pathfinder landing in 1996. More recently, many people in my circles were excited about the SpaceX Dragon launch a few months ago. But a minority of geeks excitedly watching live feeds from home doesn't compare, in my opinion, to the celebrations described above.

It's also not that we don't honor progress in any way. Formal institutions such as the Nobel prizes still do so on a regular basis. I'm talking more about ad-hoc displays of enthusiasm and admiration.

Some hypotheses

Here are a few hypotheses for why there haven't been any major celebrations of progress in the last ~50 years:

- **There haven't been as many big accomplishments.** We haven't gone back to the Moon or cured cancer. We haven't solved traffic or auto accidents. This is the stagnation hypothesis.

But what about the progress we have made? What about computers and the Internet? What about sequencing the human genome or producing insulin using genetic engineering[10]?

This leads to the second hypothesis:

- **The progress we have made hasn't been the kind that lends itself to big public celebrations.** Celebrations are generally for big, visible achievements that were completed at a defined point and that the public could easily understand. Computers and the Internet were not obviously about to change the world when they were invented, and they did so gradually over decades. The human genome was big science news but too removed from immediate practical benefit to cause dancing in the streets.

Similar explanations seem to apply to achievements in the past. For instance, in contrast to the polio vaccine, I can't remember reading about any celebrations of Edward Jenner's smallpox vaccine. The concept of vaccines (and even inoculation, the technique that preceded vaccination) was too new and too controversial. It took time for everyone to believe and accept that the vaccine worked. A century and a half later, after the germ theory was established and there were many clear successes of fighting disease with science, the public was ready to celebrate the polio vaccine.

Take another example, the Haber-Bosch process[11]. This was certainly one to celebrate, but I don't recall any parades or fireworks for it. Again, it seems perhaps too technical and removed from what the general public could get excited about.

- **People celebrate things differently now, maybe in less formal and public ways.** As noted, the ticker-tape parades in NYC waned after the mid-1960s. In an era of telecommunications, maybe people don't have as much of a need to get together in large groups? Maybe 21st-century celebration takes the form of something getting ten million likes on Facebook?

I have a hard time buying this one. We still hold parades for sports championships, launch fireworks for the Olympics, and gather in large groups for New Year's Eve. I think there is still a psychological need for big, public celebrations.

- **We just don't appreciate progress as much as we used to.** I'm not sure we need this hypothesis, in that I think the first two explain all of the observations so far. But I believe it, because it matches a broader trend of waning enthusiasm and growing skepticism and even antagonism towards progress. As a thought experiment, can you imagine Presidential speeches and a brass band at the opening of a bridge today?

What will happen for future achievements?

OK, you might say, bridges have become commonplace. What if it wasn't a bridge, but the first space elevator? Would that be met with celebration? Or opposition? Or a yawn?

Or, take a less sci-fi example: How will we greet the COVID-19 vaccine, when it arrives hopefully in the next year or two? Will people "ring bells, honk horns, blow whistles, fire salutes, drink toasts, hug children, and forgive enemies"? Will they "name schools, streets, hospitals, and newborn infants" after the creator?

Or what if Elon Musk succeeds with a manned mission to Mars? When the first Martian astronauts return, will they go on world tour like Armstrong, Aldrin, and Collins?

I don't know. Maybe! It will be interesting to see.

Endnotes

(1) Stephen E. Ambrose. Nothing Like It In the World: The Men Who Built the Transcontinental Railroad 1863-1869. 2000.

(2) David McCullough. The Great Bridge: The Epic Story of the Building of the Brooklyn Bridge. 1972.

(3) https://rootsofprogress.org/smallpox-and-vaccines

(4) David M. Oshinsky. Polio: An American Story. 2005.

(5) Steven Pinker. Enlightenment Now: The Case for Reason, Science, Humanism, and Progress. 2018.

(6) Wikipedia. List of ticker-tape parades in New York City.

(7) Wikipedia. File:Apollo 11 ticker tape parade 2.jpg.

(8) https://twitter.com/jasoncrawford/status/1294082152049434624

(9) https://twitter.com/Noahpinion/status/1294133448337063936

(10) https://americanhistory.si.edu/collections/search/object/ nmah_1000967

(11) https://rootsofprogress.org/turning-air-into-bread

Published in the United States of America
by LessWrong Press.
Berkeley, California
LessWrong.com

Printed by Hemlock in Canada
Designed by Asimov Collective in Brooklyn, New York
ISBN: 979-8-9873880-0-6
First edition

To be in a future year's set of books, publish essays on LessWrong.com